THE TAO OF TEAM
IN PRACTICE

THE TAO OF TEAM
IN PRACTICE

A treasury of
over 150 activities and conversations
for forming and sustaining
a highly effective team

ROB STONES

THE TAO OF TEAM IN PRACTICE

A TREASURY OF
OVER 150 ACTIVITIES AND CONVERSATIONS
FOR FORMING AND SUSTAINING
A HIGHLY EFFECTIVE TEAM

First published 2020.

Author: Rob Stones

Cover Design: Jeremy Stones

Author's statement:
In my work as a School Principal, Executive Team Leader, Consultant and Executive Coach I have used many activities in creating, or helping to create, effective teams. This compendium represents a selection of those activities. Some are activities I designed and created myself. Others are activities I acquired from the work of others - or through my contacts with the worldwide network of trainers and facilitators. Whenever I remember the source or author of an activity I have acknowledged it. I apologise if I have unwittingly neglected to mention any author or designer whose work is hereby presented but not acknowledged.

For other publications by Rob Stones visit *www.futureshape.com.au*

Detailed Table of Contents

FOREWORD

This is a practitioners' manual for creating team*. It describes the Tao – the way – that team comes together and becomes productive.

Apart from a page or so at the start of each section it is not a book of advocacy for team. I am assuming that if you are reading this page you probably know that working with and through your team is critical to your success as a leader.

What this book sets out to do is to put the flesh of practical strategy, team conversation and enlightening activity on to the bare bones of the intention to form and develop an effective team.

I have worked with many school leaders who know that team is important but who discover that nowhere in their training have they acquired the armoury of activities, collaborative skills and communication practices that they need to set up and sustain team. This manual is for them.

These pages offer a smorgasbord of activity that team leaders can use to connect, energise and engage all levels of the team structures on which every school relies. There are activities related to clarifying team purpose; strategies for collegial decision-making and a host of opportunities for enhancing the communication and trust between team members. The material in these pages is designed for use by school executives working with the whole school, the executive team, or with any of the other teams that shape the energising fabric of all effective schools.

These pages also contain content that can also be used by training professionals who work in support of school teams in circumstances where the school executive decides to outsource some of this work.

*You will notice that I write about creating team rather than creating a team. This is deliberate as you will read on pages 16.

THE STRUCTURE OF THIS BOOK

'The Tao of Team' has 9 sections, each of which comprises a brief introduction with practical activities, processes and reflections that school leaders can use to create and develop the teams in their school – including the team of the whole staff.

The nine sections are:

1. Connecting Team Members with Each Other:

   Activities that can be used to connect team members with each other. Whenever there are people in the team who do not yet know each other (as so often happens when there is a change of staff), or when people in one stage or faculty will benefit from getting to know a wider group of colleagues, these activities create the connections you need.

2. Team Formation Activities:

   Activities that help team members to know and understand each more deeply and to appreciate the diversity of strengths present in the team. These activities take the connections between team members to a level where mutual understanding and appreciation begin to emerge

3. Exploring Team Diversity and Dissent:

   Effective Teams need to strike a balance between group identity and the strength that comes from the gathering of diverse minds and talents. These practices enable teams to manage and understand the importance of individual contribution in a team environment. Sometimes activities in this section will need to be tackled after team purpose is established; at other times shared purpose will only emerge after team members understand the need for agreeable disagreement!

4. Creating Team Purpose and Expectation:

   Establishing Team Purpose and Direction are priorities in any team that will need to work together cohesively. Discussion about mutual expectations and about framing team-member agreement about practices are included here. Clarity of team purpose is the 'glue' that holds the team together and allows team members to express strong opinions in the service of that purpose.

5. Team Decision-making:

   When a team of people work together, the way that they deliberate and the manner in which they make decisions will affect the way that the team functions. These varied practices promote collegial decision-making, enhance commitment and establish the team ethos you need.

6. Team Meeting Starters:

   School teams often gather at the end of a busy day or at other times when team members have difficulty switching from their individual responsibilities to the work of the team. These meeting starters provide vehicles for transition.

7. Team Learning, Coaching and Capacity Building:

   Team effectiveness depends on far more that the capabilities of individual team members. Teams learn to work together with increased effectiveness when the team is coached, when they adopt reflective self-evaluation and where team learning is provided.

8. Team Energisers:

   Another way of switching on attention for a meeting or training is to use simple energisers that changes the emotional or physiological state of team members. These can be used to start a session, to energise an otherwise dry meeting or presentation, or simply to give everyone a 'lift'.

9. Team Adjournments and transitions:

   The final group of activities are those that can be used for team celebrations, reflections and closure.

The detailed table of contents from pages 7 to 12 will help you to navigate the repertoire activities.

Some NOTES on CREATING TEAM

Team is created and sustained deliberately.

The outline for this intentional and systematic process were sketched by Ralph Tuckman in his respected model of team formation. Tuckman's model argued that team is created successfully in four phases. Phases that he described as: Forming, Storming, Norming and Performing.

The stages or cycle of team development:
Based on a model by Ralph Tuckman

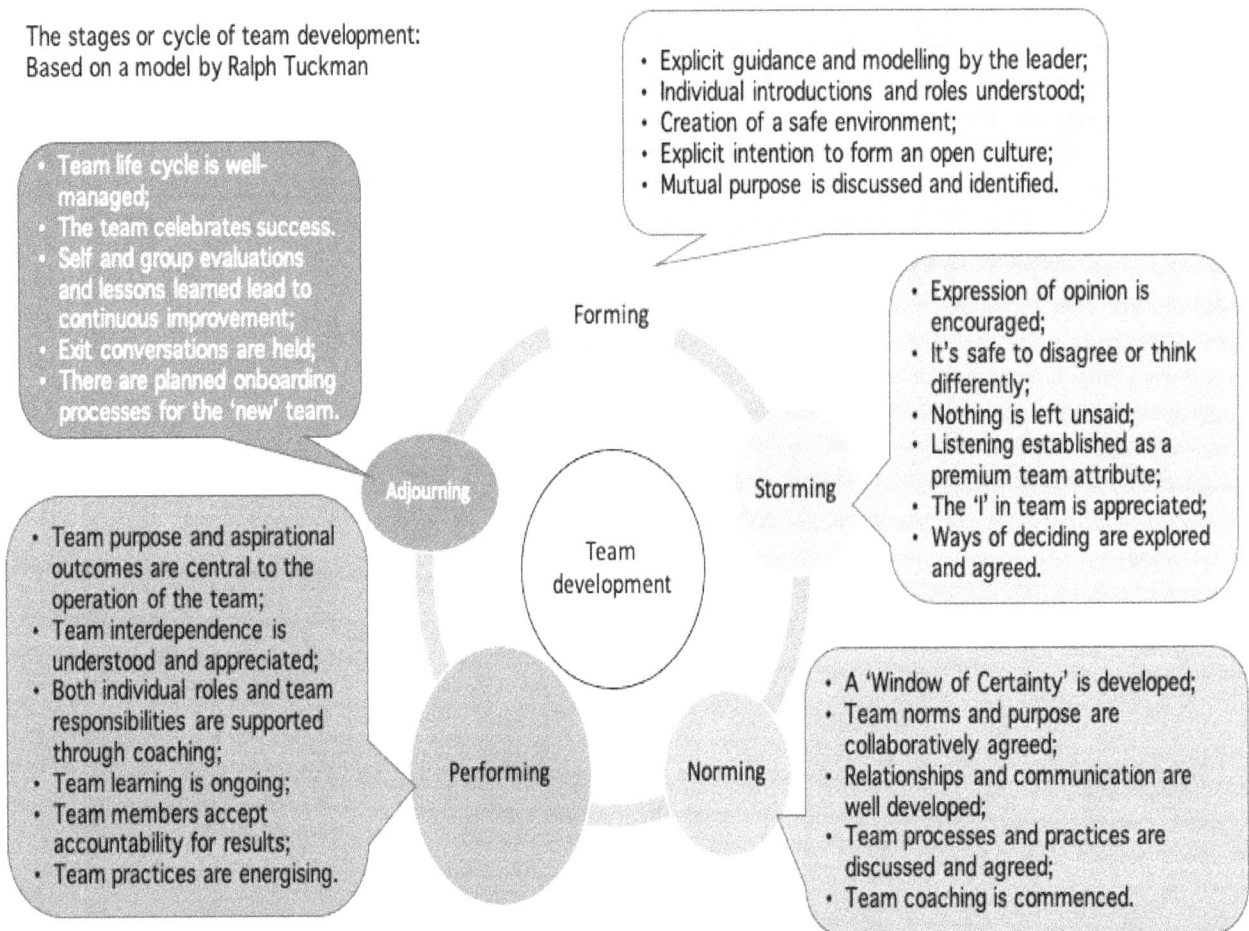

- Explicit guidance and modelling by the leader;
- Individual introductions and roles understood;
- Creation of a safe environment;
- Explicit intention to form an open culture;
- Mutual purpose is discussed and identified.

- Team life cycle is well-managed;
- The team celebrates success.
- Self and group evaluations and lessons learned lead to continuous improvement;
- Exit conversations are held;
- There are planned onboarding processes for the 'new' team.

Forming

Adjourning

Team development

Storming

- Expression of opinion is encouraged;
- It's safe to disagree or think differently;
- Nothing is left unsaid;
- Listening established as a premium team attribute;
- The 'I' in team is appreciated;
- Ways of deciding are explored and agreed.

- Team purpose and aspirational outcomes are central to the operation of the team;
- Team interdependence is understood and appreciated;
- Both individual roles and team responsibilities are supported through coaching;
- Team learning is ongoing;
- Team members accept accountability for results;
- Team practices are energising.

Performing

Norming

- A 'Window of Certainty' is developed;
- Team norms and purpose are collaboratively agreed;
- Relationships and communication are well developed;
- Team processes and practices are discussed and agreed;
- Team coaching is commenced.

Although others have refined Tuckman's model, the basis of his insight is sound. His four phases provide the framework for this manual, though as you will see I have embellished them with detail and with the addition of an adjournment phase. In a school, because team is always being formed and re-formed with the rhythm of staff turnover, the process is inevitably ongoing. Team evolves if we continue to develop it - or declines when it is taken-for-granted and neglected.

The book has been loosely based on Tuckman's framework in this way:

Phase	Purpose	Chapter
Formation	Team members meet and get to know each other. They begin the process of understanding and appreciating each other's ideas and opinions.	• Team Introductions. • Team Formation.
Storming	At the point at which differences emerge, conflict is deliberately encouraged and explored Team members work out how to disagree agreeably.	• Exploring Team Diversity and Dissent.
Norming	Team norms, protocols and mutual trust are established. Key to this phase is sufficient conversation to negotiate predictable expectations.	• Team Norms and Commitments. • Team decision making.
Performing	The team is operating cohesively and collaboratively. They are learning and developing together. Team goals are achieved.	• Team meeting starters. • Team learning and Coaching. • Team Energisers.
Adjourning	Team members change. The team and its leaders create celebrations of success and initiate closure activity. Onboarding for the next phase is commenced.	• Team reflection and closure.

You may have noticed that I write about creating team, not creating _a_ team. This is a purposeful idiosyncrasy. I am using this form of words for emphasis.

A team is not the collective noun for the group of people who have executive roles or who are members of the same stage or faculty. Being a team member is much than the passive identification of a group to which members belong as a result of their role. Team must be formed - created through deliberate processes.

Creating '_a_ team' misleadingly suggests the construction of an entity consisting of people who work together. It supports the erroneous presupposition that there can be an entity 'the team' to which team members are simply added or subtracted by the nature of their job or position. This way of thinking about team neglects the need to create a shared identity defined by mutual intention, values and commitment.

The reality is that creating team brings with it the imperative that _teaming_ (a very participatory activity) is central to the project of creating team. There can be no team without teaming; without the willing participation of team members to enter this distinctive relationship.

The activity, communication and cohesion required of effective school teams goes far beyond conventional organisational and decision-making practice. It's not that conventional meeting procedure with thoughtfully prepared agendas and predictable processes is not important to effective team performance. It is central to it. However, the productivity and value of meetings, agendas and decisions are dependent on the mutual understanding, level of trust and personal commitment of team members.

It is building reciprocal trust; appreciation of each other; learning together and the ability to engage in productive conflict that are supplements that transform a work group into a team.

PAGE STRUCTURE

Almost every page of this manual is presented with a predictable structure:

The Purpose of the activity describes heads the page.

Next is listed any **Equipment** needed for the activity (if no equipment is required, this heading is omitted).

The Process of the activity forms the central part of the page.

Most pages ends with **Reflective Questions**. These are central to the process of team learning and improvement.

Introducing Team Members to Each Other

During my 50 years as an educator I have been invited to join and participate in many teams. There have been far too few of them in which any deliberate attempt was made to introduce team members to each other in any meaningful way.

The two most common strategies used are these:

1. Team members wear name tags. [Note – name tags were invented by people who prefer to avoid real human connection]. With name tags there is no need to even remember anyone's name! Moreover there are few things less comfortable than peering at tiny writing on the chests of other people that you hardly know.
2. The Team Leader asks: "Do you know everyone?" and if anyone responds in the negative, other people quickly say their names.

These are not useful introductions for people who will share the mutual responsibilities and roles of team members. Working together collaboratively requires a deep level of relatedness. If we are going to connect with people; understand them and work together productively, more than naming is required.

All of the introduction practices listed here will provide team members with information that goes beyond merely the names of team members. Through these activities team members can also get a sense of how each individual sees the world; observe their colleagues under a little pressure; hear something of the priorities in their lives and get a sense of what it will be like to work with them.

Having used these practices in countless situations I am always gratified to hear from team members how useful and insightful they found the activities. I am certain that you will have the same experience.

Mal's Name Game

(With thanks and appreciation to Dr Malcolm Davies from whom I learned this way of introducing team members to each other).

Purpose: Introducing people in a way that helps everyone to learn names very quickly and under pressure.

Equipment: Participants sit in a circle of chairs.

Process:
1. Participants sit in a circle.
2. A brief introduction 'round' is held: each person says their name (the name they want everyone to use) and one interesting fact about themselves.
3. After the first round, the first person again says their name. The next person continues, but after saying their own name, they repeat the first person's name.
4. Th activity continues with each person saying their own name and also the names of the others who have gone before (each person will be adding one more name).
5. Reassure people - as they have to say more and more names - that it's ok if they get stuck. Encourage the others to jump in to help if anyone gets stuck.
6. Continue round the circle for several round so that everyone should be hearing the names of group members repeatedly and all have a turn at naming everyone in the group.

(Variation: after step 2, the first person names as many people as they can remember (with a little help from team members). When they get stuck the next person continues … and so on until every team member can name everyone else).

Reflective Questions:
- What did you learn about the other members of the team?
- What questions would you like to ask any member of the team?

Rob's Name Game
A variation of Mal's name game.

Purpose:
To quickly introduce team members to each other - some of whom have just met for the first time, but who will work together during the forthcoming period.

Equipment: Participants sit in a circle of chairs.

Process:
1. The team leader models by introducing himself or herself with their first name and something interesting / memorable / different / significant about them.
2. Each person in the group then introduces them self in the same way proceeding in a clockwise direction around the circle.
3. A second round of introductions is modelled. This time each person (beginning with the facilitator) says their first name accompanied by an alliterative adjective (e.g. Reflective Rob; Amiable Angela) As far as possible these descriptions should be true.
4. After these 2 rounds volunteers are called for to name everyone in the circle without further inputs. (prompts from others in the group are allowed). Someone is always prepared to give it a try!
5. After a couple of volunteers have done their best (with suitable applause for their willingness to make the attempt) participants are asked to change seats. The instruction is given to: "go and sit with someone who is most like you" (or "least like you", or "someone that you are curious about").
6. When they sit together the new partners are asked to introduce them self to each other and then go around the group identifying each person. If they forget another person's name it is OK to go and ask!
7. Further calls for volunteers to name everyone in the group are made. The group are told that everyone is expected to do this, alone or in pairs, so participants become increasingly willing to take the risk (and, or course, the more they hear people's names, the more confident they become).
8. After 10-15 minutes of volunteer efforts and working in pairs, group members will be able to name each other and know something about most members of the group.

Reflective Question: Who would you like to know more about?

The McFadden name game
As demonstrated to me by Judy Mcfadden

Purpose:

To introduce group members to each other, learn something of their self-perception and history and usually gain an insight into their values.

This is a good activity to begin an in-depth workshop, or when a new professional team first meets.

Process:

1. Group members each have 3-5 minutes to talk about their names: both their first names and family name and to explain what their names mean to them.
2. Other members of the group have an opportunity for a maximum of 2 questions between them.
3. Emotional intelligence is encouraged!

Reflective Questions.

When everyone has introduced them self the facilitator may ask:

- What do we have in common OR what diversity did you notice?
- How will what we have learned about each other help us to work together?
- What else would we like to know?

Participants could be encouraged to talk individually to those who are most like them/least like them; to those with whom have interests in common or with those who seem very different!

Cartography

Purpose: To introduce team members to each other. To give the team a sense of the geographical and cultural diversity of their origins.

Process:

1. Team members place themselves on an imaginary map laid out in the room to represent the country or region they identify as their birthplace or origin. It's usually easiest to start like this:

   a. find out who was born and grew up the furthest from the place of the activity and use that to determine the 'scale' of the map.

   b. Determine which direction is North.

2. Team members arrange themselves on the points of the compass from 'this place' and the distance themselves from there according to the scale established.

3. Ask everyone to share one important value they acquired from the place where they grew up and one short story about that place or region.

Reflective Questions:

Ask everyone to consider the ways in which the diversity (or similarity) of the team may affect their conversation and decision making. Discuss in small groups and share any important insights.

Unique and Shared

Purpose: An introduction activity.

Equipment: None - but a large open space is helpful.

Process:

1. Ask team members to form groups of 4-5 people at random. I often use clumps (next page) to lead into this.
2. Give the groups 5 minutes to discover as many things as possible that they have in common, plus at least one interesting fact about every group member that is unique within the group.
3. Ask each group to report to the whole group on what they had in common. As each common characteristic is shared, people from other groups who share the same commonality raise their hands and shout 'me too!'.
4. Everyone has 5 minutes to mingle and see if anyone else in the whole group shares any other of their 'unique' characteristics.

Reflective Questions

In small groups (3) participants discuss what they have found out about team members - and what their discoveries mean to them.

Clumps

Purpose: To move people into different sized groups in order to begin the process of finding out about all of their team members. This is a very useful activity whenever you want the team to work in random groups.

Process:

The team leader or activity facilitator calls out a number and /or a description for each clump. E.g:

- Clump with 3 team members whose eyes are the same colour;
- Clump with 4 people who you know very little about;
- Please get into clumps of # (any number);
- Find a clump of 3 with a travel experience in common;
- Clump with one other persona with a similar taste in music;

Each time a clump is formed team members are given a few minutes to find out more about each other.

Reflective Questions:

- What surprised you about that activity?
- Is there anyone that you have not yet met?
- What have you found you have in common with other team members?

Quotes

Purpose: This is a formation activity that is one step beyond simple introductions. It enables participants to share opinions, beliefs and values as well as information about themselves.

Equipment: Prepared quotes on slips of paper or index cards. The quotes can be about leadership or about working together or motivation. These are easy to source from the web. An open space is needed

Process:

1. Prepare the quotes about leadership or working together or motivation. These should be written or printed on individual slips of paper or card. There should be about 25% more quotes than the number of participants in the group.

2. The papers with the quotes are placed in a pile in the centre of the room.

3. Each participant picks up one quote, then mingles with the group to find a partner that they want to know more about. They share quotes and each says what it means to them and why it is important.

4. After 2 minutes (keep it short) ask pairs to move on and find a new partner. They can either take their own quote; change quotes with their previous partner; or pick a new quote from the pile (leaving their 'old' quote in the pile).

5. Repeat for 10-15 minutes.

Reflective Questions:

In small groups (3-4) participants can:
- Discuss any themes they noticed;
- Identify quotations they feel may have particular significance for this group;
- Discuss what the activity revealed about group diversity.

Pinwheel

Purpose:
- To introduce team members or training participants to each other.
- To practise listening attentively to team members.

Process:
1. The leader asks each team member to introduce themselves in turn around the circle in 3 successive pinwheels (circuits of the group).
2. If even one of the participants is new to the team, then every person should begin with their name in each pinwheel.
3. The first pinwheel should be very general and non-threatening - for example:
   a. Tell us about your favourite food or favourite place;
   b. What you do for recreation;
   c. The books you like to read (movies you like to watch).
4. The second pinwheel should begin to touch upon the subject of the meeting or the work of the team. The following examples might be used if the team is going to discuss the effectiveness of their team in leading the school:
   a. How you define leadership;
   b. A colleague or a leadership practice you admire;
   c. What you see as the challenges of your job.
5. The final pinwheel should prompt participants to express their opinions about the subject to be discussed, or the purpose of the meeting. These examples again come from a leadership team meeting – this one the first of the year:
   a. What would you like us to achieve as a team this year?
   b. Are there some things we should discuss as a team that are usually left unsaid?
   c. What do you bring to the team that we should tap into?

Reflective Questions: The discussion after a pinwheel usually arises quite naturally from the contributions of team members. It's important that the team leader picks up any common threads from the second and third pinwheel and either initiates discussion immediately or at a convenient future time.

Three Truths and One Lie

Purpose:
An introductory activity that encourages mingling, discussion and exploration – it enables team members to find out interesting information about each other that is not usually shared.

Equipment: Index cards or slips of paper for each person. Pens.

Process:
1. Team members / participants are asked to write, on a 6x4 'About Me' card, four interesting or surprising things about themselves. Three of these will be true. One will be fabricated but believable.
2. Team members mingle and when they encounter each other offer their 'about me' cards to each other.
3. They ask each other questions about the four 'facts' on the card they are shown in order to work out which of these truths in, in fact, a lie.
4. When they think they know, participants identify the 'one lie' about the other that they have inferred from the conversation. If they guess correctly their partner admits it. If they have **not** guessed correctly the partner shakes their head but does not reveal the 'lie'.
5. Participants continue to mingle until all (or at least most) have had a chance to pair off and guess at each other's truths and lies.
6. Participants stand in a circle and each person in turn identifies the 'lie' they told by saying "I never ….etc.".

Reflective Questions
Group leader asks the whole group - what did we find out about each other that was:
- Surprising?
- Predictable?
- Useful?

Did we learn anything about what we have in common (or about what our differences are) that will help us to work together constructively?

Who is in the room?

Purpose: To 'introduce participants or team members to each other. This activity can be used either when there are several people new to the group OR when the group's knowledge about each other is mostly role related and it would be helpful if team members shared something more about themselves.

Process

1. Team members sit in a circle. The team leader or facilitator asks questions such as the following:
   - Do we have any parents in the room?
   - Do we have grandparents in the room?
   - Do we have readers in the room?
   - Do we have poets/artists in the room?
   - Do we have athletes in the room?
   - Do we have champions in the room?
   - Do we have coffee lovers in the room?
   - Do we have chefs in the room?
   - Do we have investors in the room?

If team members self-identify as belonging to the category named, they wave, cheer or shout 'That's me!". Any team members can ask for more details about what is revealed by others.

(At any point the team leader can invite team members to take over asking the questions).

2. After several rounds, team members are asked to clump with other team members who:
   a. Have common interests;
   b. Are very different;
   c. Have not yet identified themselves;
   d. They would like to talk to.

Note – don't let the activity go on too long if it's only a meeting starter.

Debriefing:

Not usually necessary though the team leader might ask participants sitting next to each other: What did you learn about your colleagues that was surprising? Insightful? Helpful?

Partner Introductions

Based on leadership learning research by the Centre of Creative Leadership (USA).

Purpose:
Helps team members get to know each other; as a check-in; when new members have joined the team.

Process:
Pair off with a team-member that you feel you could learn more about.
Introduce yourself in the following way:

Taking just 5 minutes each, please share:
- o Your name and one interesting biographical detail;
- o One illustration or example from **each** of the following dimensions of your career history.

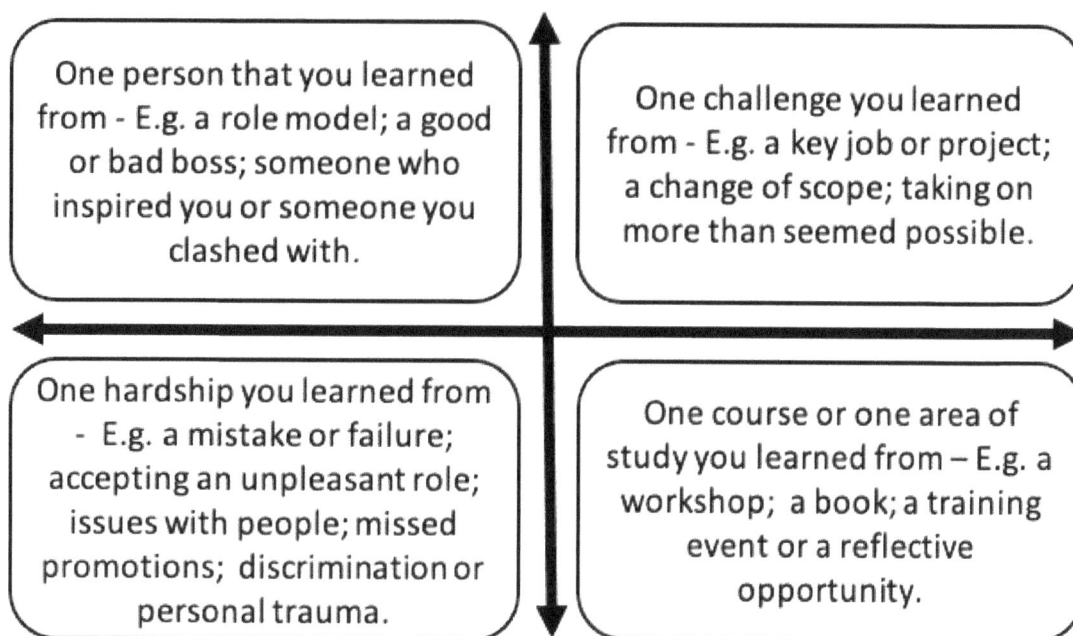

One person that you learned from - E.g. a role model; a good or bad boss; someone who inspired you or someone you clashed with.

One challenge you learned from - E.g. a key job or project; a change of scope; taking on more than seemed possible.

One hardship you learned from - E.g. a mistake or failure; accepting an unpleasant role; issues with people; missed promotions; discrimination or personal trauma.

One course or one area of study you learned from – E.g. a workshop; a book; a training event or a reflective opportunity.

Return to the circle and introduce your partner, using the same the format - but keeping each presentation to two minutes.

Reflective Questions: In whole group: what did we learn about each other that was new?

Note: You can use this format as a different way of checking-in - using any of the other check-in starters or questions.

Section Two

Team Formation Processes

A recent research study[1] showed that the quality and effectiveness of interaction between the members of effective teams is characterised by regular face-to-face communication between most (if not all) team members - both within and outside formal meetings. The levels of communication and connection between these team members is comprehensive and inclusive. That's quite different from the patterns of less effective teams where the interaction is less frequent and where there are very weak connections between many team members.

These high levels of communication and mutual interdependence are never accidental. The habit of frequent and fruitful communication has to be encouraged by deliberate team formation. The leaders of productive teams initiate and encourage the development of trust and mutual respect - and they are prepared to invest time to create what they want.

We know that team members trust those of their colleagues who are predictable; respectful; who listen to (and value) their opinions; have a positive intent and an obvious commitment to a common purpose. They invest the time to talk with and encourage each other when they come to know they can contribute to each other's effectiveness and can negotiate in a way that respects difference.

How do team members develop this level of relationship with their team colleagues?

The answer is that they spend time talking with each other; learning together; listening to each other; intentionally attempting to understand the values and opinions of their colleagues, and by learning and using perceptual agility – especially 2nd perceptual position.

These interactions cannot - and do not - happen by chance. They are created purposefully by team leaders who recognise that the ways high levels of team communication and trust are developed necessitates the investment of time.

This is not something that team leaders only need do in the early stages of the life of the team. Formation is never complete. Teams change, team members change, individuals within a team learn and develop, new issues emerge. There is a real sense in which a team is always forming, returning to storming and re-norming in order to become relevant to its purpose.

This section contains a selection of activities that help the team leader to form the team and develop the individual and team capabilities needed.

From the reading, research and experience that comes from a lifetime of working with team (both successfully and unsuccessfully) these six, perhaps surprising, capabilities stand out:
1. Ability to formulate a shared purpose;
2. A commitment to encouraging open and comprehensive communication;
3. Appreciation and encouragement of team member individuality and autonomy;
4. The capacity to identify the Interdependence of team members;
5. Thoughtful use of consensus decision-making;
6. The ability of the team leader to encourage constructive dispute and deep thinking.

The thirteen formation activities in this section help the team to address the first four of these capabilities.

[1] *Alex Pentland, The New Science of Creating Great Teams, Harvard Business Review 2012.*

On-Boarding the New Team
(Developed from a process conceived and recommended by Ruth Wageman[1])

Purpose: To create a process through which school leadership teams re-commit annually to their shared purpose and working together. One of the potential weaknesses of school executive teams is that they are usually assembled from those in executive roles and so membership is regarded as 'automatic'. This process challenges the assumption that people are team members by right and asserts that joining the executive team is a deliberate decision that involves strong commitment. (Note: This process can be used for other teams as well.)

Process:
1. Toward the end of each school year, the executive team holds a completion ceremony to celebrate the events of the year past. (see *Team Adjournments* in Section Nine).

2. Shortly thereafter, or at the very beginning of the new school year, prospective leadership team members are interviewed by the Team Leader and invited to become members of the 'new' executive team. They are reminded of the purpose of the Team, asked about their commitment to this purpose and (if they are committed) invited to join the team for the next year. They will understand that membership of the team entails an obligation to develop trusting and interdependent relationships with other team members.

    Note: Staff whose role would normally entail membership of this team, but who are unwilling to commit to team purpose, will negotiate individual arrangements with the Team Leader. In practice, most potential team members will be willing to make the commitment but there has to be a separate arrangement for those who will not. Usually this arrangement allows them to be excused from executive meetings and entails a negotiated reporting relationship. It's important that the door is always left open: if they change their minds and decide to commit to the team they are welcomed and included.

3. To note the formation of the team a formal commitment 'ceremony' is held. The members of the team for the coming year dedicate themselves to the ongoing purpose of the team and are given a formal recognition of that dedication. This can be a symbol, badge, certificate or team shirt – whatever is deemed appropriate and meaningful.

4. Team members co-create or (if previously created) re-commit to the Team Norms or 'Window of Certainty' that provide the direction for the team. The Norms or W.O.C. are

an ever-present artefact that symbolises team cohesion. These are printed for team members and are frequently used as a standard against which to evaluate team performance.

Reflective Questions: The main use of debriefing in these circumstances is to provide opportunities to clarify the rationale for making executive team membership voluntary. Questions such as these are relevant and thought-provoking:

- What is the difference between being told that you are a member of the team (or simply assuming that you must be a member) and being invited to join?
- What would be the effect on team activity if staff who do not want to be included are forced to be team members?
- Given the amount of time that we spend working together as a team, is it important that we do so willingly?
- How does knowing that we are voluntarily making a commitment of time and energy affect our willingness to work hard to achieve outcomes we will be proud of?

[1] *Ruth Wageman, Author of "Senior Leadership Teams" Wageman, Nunes, Burruss and Hackman; 2008.*

Perceptual Positions

The Perceptual Positions were developed by the NLP community from pioneering work by Gregory Bateson on the different perspectives from which we can view the world.

Purpose: To introduce the use of perceptual positions to the group so that it can be used as a key instrument for focusing the attention of the team when problem-solving or making decisions.

Equipment: A single page describing the 4 perceptual positions (next page)

Process:
1. The Team Leader introduces the 4 perceptual positions using the simplified presentation on the next page. He or she emphasises that each of the positions is a different way of paying attention to people and events.
2. The team is asked to express their opinion about a current topic of interest to the team. It could be about a change initiative that is in progress; a curriculum or pedagogical issue being considered by the school; a system change that is in the offing, or any topic that usually elicits some variety of opinion (such as 'how to teach students to be more responsible').
3. The team works in pairs:
   a. Everyone is encouraged to offer a 1st position opinion on the topic chosen. Team members are invited to share their personal opinions.
   b. Next, everyone is asked to articulate a 2nd position from what they have just heard, paying attention to any point of view which is very different from their own.
   c. In 3rd position team members are invited to be analytic and objective. They might use a metaphor or analogy to describe the differences between statements made in the first two parts of this activity.
   d. In 4th they attempt to be as sage and insightful as possible with a focus not only on the consequences of a course of action but on the consequences of those consequences!
4. The team discusses the effort required to truly pay attention in each position.

Reflective Questions:
- In what ways could systematic use of the perceptual positions help us to make good decisions as a team?
- Which perceptual position should we be in when we are listening to each other?
- How will we use the perceptual positions in other contexts?

Perceptual Positions - illustrated

4th

system

4th Perceptual Position. In this position I am paying attention as a leader – concerned only for what is best for the school. In this position I am attending to long-term consequences for staff and students

3rd

observer

3rd Perceptual Position. In this position I am paying attention as an objective observer - seeing the situation analytically. In 3rd position I am detached and diagnostic in describing what is happening.

2nd

other

2nd Perceptual Position. In this position I am paying attention to the thoughts, attitudes and beliefs of someone else. In 2nd position I am empathic – trying to understand the world as it seems to someone else.

1st

me

1st Perceptual Position. In this position I am paying attention to my own thoughts, attitudes and beliefs and expressing my own opinions. In first position I am assertive and often try to be persuasive.

Team Norms: What should ours be?

Adapted from: *Senior Leadership Teams* Wageman, Nunes, Burruss and Hackman; *2008.*

Purpose: The best teams, according to Ruth Wageman[1], have norms to which they hold each other accountable. These norms (or conventions) should regulate the way that team members conduct themselves, both in their meetings and in their interaction and communication with the staff they lead. Wageman and her colleagues suggest that, as a minimum, senior teams should have team norms related to:

○ Commitment – Acting as though your role in the team is critical to the school's success. Demonstrating accountability to the team.

○ Transparency – Anything that affects the performance of the team or communication with staff should be on the table.

○ Participation – Every team member must honour their own voice and be prepared to speak their truth boldly.

○ Integrity – Everything that is said and done in the team, and all commitments made in the team, must be identical with what is communicated to those outside the team.

Equipment: Copies of these two pages

Process:

1. The team works in 4 groups – each group tackling ONE of the commitment areas: Commitment, Transparency, Participation and Integrity.

2. Each group proposes a team norm or norms related to their areas (10 minutes). If necessary, they can discuss the 'sample team norms' (shown below) to stimulate their thinking.

3. The norms created by each group are circulated and edited as they are viewed by each group.

4. The revised norms are recirculated and adopted when agreed (see the Consensus Decision-making pages).

Reflective Questions:

- Are we all prepared to accept the proposed norms?
- If any of us believe the norms are not being followed, what action should be taken and by whom?

Once the norms are established, the team can self-valuate against one aspect of the team norms they have established.

For example:
- How did our meeting today contribute to our purpose/intended outcomes?
- Which of our norms did our meeting exemplify today? Were there any we should have paid more attention to?
- How well did we live by our beliefs and values in the way we conducted ourselves and made decisions today?

Example team norms (to stimulate thinking):

1. Come to our meetings on time and prepared to make a thoughtful contribution. If at any time you do not feel our discussions are important or relevant, say so immediately.
2. Contribute fully. Say everything in our meetings that you have to say about each topic discussed. If you don't say it here, please don't say it anywhere else.
3. Participate as fully as you can in every decision. If you are not clear about what we are deciding please say so. If you are not clear about how the decision is being made, please ask questions until you are.
4. Once a decision is made (even if we do not come to consensus and the decision is that of the majority or is the Principal's casting decision) it becomes the decision of the team, and it is never acceptable to disclaim it or say to others that you did not agree.
5. Our meeting is held in the meeting room. There are no 'car park' meetings.
6. You have just as great a responsibility to listen to others as to speak up yourself. It is your job as a team member to attempt to understand your team colleagues. It is especially important to understand positions that you do not find agreeable. If you don't understand, ask questions.
7. If you think there are assumptions being made, or that a discussion is being clouded by underlying agendas, please question or challenge these.
8. It is expected that we will often have to work hard to come to agreement. When we do not all agree, we will remember that team unity is important enough to our school for us to be unfailingly courteous and respectful towards each other.
9. Our meetings will be well planned, and we will stick to the published agenda. The items that will have the most impact on student performance will always be dealt with first.

[1] *Ruth Wageman, Author of "Senior Leadership Teams" Wageman, Nunes, Burruss and Hackman; 2008.*

Ideal Me As Leader
(based on an activity created by Tom Siebold)

Purpose: To create a norm for ideal leadership by comparing each person's ideal of leadership behaviour with what they actually do. An insightful activity for Leadership Team members but also for members of teaching teams who are reflecting on their classroom leadership versus management.

Equipment: One copy of the 'Do versus Prefer to Do' Table (next page).

Process
1. Ask participants to reflect on how they actually use their time on a daily basis.
2. Then ask them to complete the 'DO .v. Prefer to DO table on the next page.
3. Follow up with a small group discussion addressing the questions:
   - Individually, did we discover that our leadership behaviour is congruent with what we believe we should be doing to be most influential as leaders?
   - As a group are there some behaviours we believe we should do LESS of, and some we should do MORE of?
   - Are there some ways that we can coach each other and hold each other accountable for bringing us closer to the ideal?
   - Each small group summarises their discussion and conclusion for the whole group.

Reflective Questions: (for the whole group)

- As an ideal or 'Norm' for this group, are there some priorities for us in terms of the leadership behaviours we model for our staff (or students)?
- What are we prepared to do to optimise the time we spend on useful or ideal leadership behaviours?

The 'DO .v. Prefer to DO' Table*

Think about your daily interaction with the people whom you lead (staff or students). Using the list of behaviours in the table below, work out how much time (as % of time available) you generally devote to each behaviour. Put this in the column headed 'DO'.

Then in the 'PREFER' column, estimate what you feel would be ideal % of time (or energy) spent on each activity.

Behaviour	DO % of interactive time spent on each behaviour	PREFER Ideally % of time you would prefer to devote to each behaviour
Giving Information		
Giving Instructions		
Coaching or Mentoring		
Inspiring or Persuading		
Collaborating with others		
Listening		
Reflection & Self-Evaluating		
Observing		
Reprimanding or Praising		
Negotiating or Resolving Conflicts		
Encouraging		
Other?		

*Note that you can also use this table as a personal reflection activity whenever you would like to conduct a personal review of how you spend your time.

Walk and Talk Reflection

Purpose:

To encourage reflective practice through collegial conversation and to enhance levels of trust and understanding between team members. Can be used before or after meetings or professional learning activities, or as a regular feature of professional reflective practice.

Process:

1. Before during or after staff or leadership meetings professional learning days, participants share their thinking with a professional colleague.
2. Reflective partners may be chosen either for the particular meeting or training or on an ongoing basis to encourage regular deep reflection.
3. The reflective partners walk and talk for 6 to 8 minutes, sharing their recent learning or their perceptions of their day-to-day professional experience.
4. When the whole group re-convenes, participants are encouraged to share any insights and ideas from their personal reflection either in small groups or with the whole group (or both).

Reflective Comments and Activity:

- The de-brief is incorporated in the activity.
- A facilitator might ask probing or observant questions to deepen the understanding of the individual and group.

TRUST Conversations

Purpose:

In the leadership context, trust is not built by accident or without thoughtful and deliberate process. This is one way of creating trust-building conversations.

Process:

1. Team members are randomly selected to work together (draw names or numbers from a hat; step forward and partner with the person who is closest; or choose or any other pairing process).
2. Each pair takes turns to initiate a structured conversation:
   a. Tell me about your role?
   b. What's most important to you about your role?
   c. What would you change about your work if you could?
   d. What are your most noble values?
3. When the partner is answering the questions, the role of the partner is to listen with understanding using 2nd perceptual position.
4. At the end of each conversation, partners share what was most important or insightful for them in listening to the other.
5. Ideally, all team members will have an opportunity to have a trust conversation with every other team member during the extended period when they are team members.

Reflective Questions.

After every trust building session the facilitator asks:

- What did you learn that was of value to you in developing trust with your partner?
- Which questions went deepest and generated the most trust?
- What did you learn that you can use with your own team or class?

The Reflective Ramble

Purpose:
Similar to the 'walk and talk' process in that participants 'ramble' with each other while they reflect on their learning or experience.

Process:
1. The process is used after an intense meeting, a deep discussion or a professional learning experience that requires reflective analysis.
2. Participants walk and talk using these prompts for their reflection:
   - What did I appreciate?
   - What have learned?
   - What was I challenged by?
   - What questions do I have?
   - What is my promise to myself about future learning?
3. Share with small or whole group as in the 'Walk and Talk Review'.

Reflection or review:

- The de-brief is incorporated in the activity.
- A facilitator might ask probing or observant questions to deepen the insights of participants.
- Other questions or comments might be added to challenge group members.

It's Obvious

Purpose: To deepen the team's understanding of each other and also to initiate discussion about how first impressions are important but can be deceptive

Process:

1. The team is asked to stand or sit in a circle.

2. Starting with the team leader, each person says three things about the person on their left:
   o Their **first** sentence starts with the words, **"It's obvious …":** this sentence should state something that is obvious to them about the person on their left.
   o The **second** sentence starts with, **"I notice …":** this sentence should state something less obvious but which they have noticed about this person.
   o The **third** sentence starts with, **"My intuition tells me that you …":** this sentence should be a guess or a spontaneous though about something the person likes or something important about them.

3. When everyone has had a turn (encourage speed!) then the team breaks into groups of 3 and 4 and talks about the significance of what is 'noticed' and 'guessed'.

Reflective Questions:
   o How can we influence what is noticed about us? (a significant question for both introverted and extraverted team members).
   o What can we say about intuition as a source of information?
   o Why do 'impressions' matter?

Follow Ball

Purpose: The purpose of the activity is made clear in the debrief. It is an activity that helps team members understand and appreciate the importance of the interdependence of the group, as well as the ways in which they can all support each other.

Equipment: Juggling Balls or Cush Balls (or any ball that is soft but has enough weight to be thrown across a circle). There should be about one ball per two team members.

Process: (The 'set-up' is complicated to write down, but quite simple in practice).

1. The team stands in a circle. Half the participants are given a ball. The leader asks team members to throw and catch the balls and to keep them moving across the circle (the ball must always be thrown across the circle not to team members who are close to you).

2. There will be chaos. Allow it to continue just long enough for many balls to be missed and dropped.

3. Pause the activity. Tell the group that we are going to set up a system to make things easier.

4. When the activity resumes ask team members to toss the ball to the person to their left and receive the ball from the person on their right. Circulate the balls round the circle using that process and using all the balls. Ask participants to notice who they pass the ball to and who they receive it from (always the same person).

5. Pause the activity again. Every second person in the circle hold up their hand (this enables the leader to check that everyone understands 'every second person'). When the leader has checked that everyone understands ask the person with their hand up to walk across the circle so that they are exactly opposite the person from whom they receive the ball.

6. Each person will now be across the circle from both the person they throw to and the person they receive from.

7. Resume the activity.

8. As the activity continues, periodically stop the group and ask questions such as:
   - What do thrower and catcher have to do to make sure that the ball is not dropped?
   - What happens when the ball is thrown to a catcher who is not ready?
   - How can the thrower make sure that the ball is easily caught?
   - Is there any way for us to improve the process so that we are all keeping the balls moving effectively and efficiently?

9. When the group has the balls circulating well (and before they get tired) stop for the debrief.

Reflective Questions:
- How is this activity a metaphor for our team and how we work together?
- What could the ball represent if we are thinking of our team? (examples might be - communication, commitments to each other, trust).
- Who is responsible for making sure that the communication between us is accurate and effective?

Many other debriefing questions are possible and can be tailored to the context of the team and any difficulties they are having at present.

It's often useful to ask team members to move into groups of 3-4 to discuss what the activity meant to them.

Wisdom Walls

(or 'Stand by your quote' – described on several online trainer sites).

Purpose: To tap into higher levels of thinking that can be accessed any time that the team addresses a problem.

Equipment: A dozen or more A3 (or larger posters) with inspiring leadership or team related quotes on them. These can be selected so that they are relevant to the situation that the team finds themselves in, or to a challenge facing the team.

Process:
1. Space the posters around the walls of the meeting room. Some examples of quotes that might be used are:

- "The best way to predict the future is to create it."   Peter Drucker
- "The manager accepts the status quo; the leader challenges it." Warren Bennis
- "Leadership is liberating people to do what is required of them in the most effective and humane way possible." Mex DePree
- "Those who hear not the music think the dancers are mad."   Chinese proverb
- "Only those who will risk going too far can possibly find out how far one can go." T.S. Eliot
- "The leader has to be a virtuoso question asker."   Lee Thayer
- "Effective Leaders leave a trail of capability in their wake." RG Pierre
- "You must be the change you wish to see in the world." Mahatma Ghandi
- "Anyone who has never made a mistake has never tried anything new." Albert Einstein.
- "The function of leadership is to produce more leaders, not more followers."   Ralph Nader
- "Good leadership consists of showing average people how to do the work of superior people." John D Rockefeller
- "Perhaps the most central characteristic of authentic leadership is the relinquishing of the impulse to dominate others." David Cooper

Google makes it relatively easy to source quotes that have the most relevance to your situation.

2. Ask people to stand by the quote that they see most relevant (or most insightful or most challenging) for the team given the situations they face.

3. Each person explains why they chose that piece of wisdom and how they see it as relevant to the current context.
4. As a group, discuss the way that following the wisdom of any of the quotes might assist with team effectiveness, or other people's perception of the team, at this time.
5. Participants may be asked to plan their next steps as a team with any of the wisdom quotations in mind.

Reflective Questions:
- How will we remind ourselves to use the wisdom we have tapped into today?
- Are there some quotations that are more relevant to the whole team than to individuals – and vice-versa?
- If we separate our work into four categories:
    - Inspiring and Influencing;
    - Building Capacity;
    - Optimising outcomes for students;
    - Communicating and co-ordination;

    Which quote or quotes could guide us in the way we address these?

'My Pet Frustration'

Purpose: For team members to learn more about the frustrations and dislikes that are depleting the energy of their team-mates. This can be very important in lifting the level of appreciation of difference and in maintaining the energy of team interaction. This is also an exercise in empathic listening and an opportunity for reflection.

Process:

1. team members choose a partner to work with.
2. Each in turn has 5 minutes to describe a situation or person that they find extremely difficult or frustrating and the ways in which this appears to affect them
   - **Note** that if a person is identified it should never be a team member who is in the room and the level of frustration should be low enough for people to feel comfortable to share.
3. The speaker has 5 minutes to talk about their frustration and what it means to them. Their partner listens in 2nd perceptual position with sensitivity and understanding. The listener does not comment or give any hint of judgement.
4. At the end of the 5-minute period the speaker thanks the listener and describes how it felt to be listened to and understood.
5. The listener then asks the speaker if they think that the dis-like they described reveals what is truly important to them (See 'Flipping' page 104). They may discuss this for a few minutes.
6. Change speaker/listener.

Reflective Questions:
- How can we use our clarity about what frustrates us to give us insights into what is really important to us?
- When might this activity be useful for us as a team?

Johari Activity

Purpose:

To provide each member of the group or team with some feedback about how they are perceived by others. The activity is based on the 'Johari Window' (created by Joseph Luft and Harrington Ingham) and is quite challenging. It's recommended that you use it either when there is relatively open communication in the group, and you want to enhance it further OR when communication is so closed that it requires drastic action to change it.

Equipment: A highlighter for each person, two copies of the *'Perceptions of Me'* page for each person (example on the next page).

Process:

1. Participants sit in a circle and are each given **two** copies of the 'Perceptions of Me' page - a list of personal values.
2. On one page, each person highlights the 10 perceptions / values that they expect that the other group members have of them. They keep that page. On the other page they write their name on the top and pass it to the person on their left.
3. All pages are circulated in a clockwise direction so that each person can provide feedback to every other participant.
4. Each person reads the name at the top of the page and then puts a star beside the 10 values or qualities that they believe are characteristic of that person. The facilitator emphasises the importance of not being influenced by the stars already on the page.
5. When all the circulated pages come back to the person whose name is on the page, he or she compares the 'stars' allocated by other group members with the qualities or values they applied to themselves.

Reflective Questions:

- Looking at your own 2 pages: What surprised you? What was as you expected? What would you like to know more about?
- If there is more information that you need, who will you get it from and how?
- Which of the personal qualities that are important to you do you need to demonstrate more clearly to group members? How will you do that? Is there a person in the group that you would trust to mentor you?
  - NOTE: Welcome discussion, but don't insist on it.

Perceptions of Me

Which values or Qualities in the following list do you believe that your colleagues will see in you? Which do you see in yourself?

Accepting
Accessible
Accommodating
Adaptable
Aggressive
Altruistic
Amenable
Ambitious
Appreciative
Approachable
Assertive
Available
Calm
Cautious
Conscientious
Cheerful
Clear
Committed
Compassionate
Composed
Compliant
Confident
Conformist
Consistent
Having Conviction
Cooperative
Courageous
Courteous
Creative
Credible
Decisive
Dependable
Determined
Diligent
Dynamic
Direct
Effective

Efficient
Empathic
Energetic
Enigmatic
Enthusiastic
Excited
Fair
Firm
Focused
Friendly
Fun
Garrulous
Generous
Grateful
Gregarious
Guiding
Harmonious
Helpful
Honest
Honourable
Humble
Impartial
Ingenious
Inquisitiveness
Inspirational
Intimidating
Have Integrity
Hard to get to know
Kind
Leadership
Logical
Loyalty
Lucid
Making a difference
Mature
Mindful
Modest
Mysterious
Obedient
Open-minded
Open communicator
Optimistic
Orderly
Organized
Original

Passive
Perceptive
Perfectionist
Perseverance
Persistent
Persuasive
Popular
Polite
Practical
Pragmatic
Have Presence
Professional
Punctual
Rational
Reasonable
Reflective
Relaxed
Reliable
Reserved
Resilient
Resistant
Resourceful
Respectful
Self-controlled
Selfless
Sensitive
Service -oriented
Sharing
Sincere
Stern
Strong
Supportive
Sympathetic
Task-focused
Team-worker
Thankful
Thorough
Trusting
Trustworthy
Truthful
Understanding
Unflappable
Warm
Wise
Witty

Photo Finish

Purpose: As a discussion starter about team planning and communication – and possible team resilience.

Equipment: A space is needed through which the whole team can walk at once. A line marking the destination end of the space. (Easy to set up on a marked basketball or netball court or any similar space).

Process:
The goal of the challenge is for the whole group to step across the end line at exactly the same time.
1. Start the team at the end of the space furthest from the line.
2. Explain that once the team begins to move, everyone must keep moving. They can slow down or speed up, but no-one can stop.
3. Planning time is allowed.
4. Once the team is given the signal to begin the activity is live!
5. If one person stops, or anyone steps across the line before or after the rest of the team, then they must all go back to the start and begin again.
6. Continue until the team is successful in crossing the line together.

Reflective Questions:
- What did this activity tell us about team planning and communication?
- Is 'near enough – good enough' an appropriate dictum for our team?
- What were the aspects of the activity that interfered with / enabled eventual success?

Section Three

Exploring Team Dissent and Diversity

These activities enhance the mutual understanding team members have of each other. They contribute to mutual honesty and eventually come to enhance trust.

The timing of these conversations is a matter of judgment:
- *Sometimes they are needed before team purpose is clarified so that all agreements are underpinned by frank exchanges of opinion;*
- *At times shared purpose is a precondition for the emergence of plain speaking and personal assertiveness;*
- *Sometimes these activities and conversations are needed when the time is ripe to emphasise the importance of a multiplicity of viewpoints.*

Without diversity - and unless team members are willing to express strong opinion and encouraged to do so - teams rarely flourish. They can become prey to easy and superficial agreements or 'groupthink'. The grinding and polishing process from which precious stones emerge is also needed for great team performance.

However, there is a conundrum here. High performing teams need to be unified behind a clear and compelling purpose - to be capable of collaboration and willing to invest their individual talents in the service of the team.

The resolution of this puzzling contradiction is the creation of a carefully balanced strategic approach to encouraging both team unity and team-member diversity. This dilemma can be resolved by managing two priorities:

    One: the members of the team must be brought together by the team's purpose and common direction (next chapter). This is logically the first step - though often clear purpose only emerges when dissent and personal honesty have been encouraged.

    Two: the team leader must model and encourage diversity, endorse creative conflict and show the way towards agreeable approaches to disagreement.

At the core of this balancing act is recognition by the team leader that he or she is not the proprietor of truth. This should be made explicit, never assumed. Warren Bennis' injunction that: "the first duty of the follower is to speak truth to power" is only effective when it has been endorsed and modelled by the team leader or Principal. The Leader who wants to get the best from the team around them, and indeed the best from themselves, has to welcome truth telling and the contrary opinions of team members. Only despots welcome loyalty above all else.

The corporate memory in education passes on many stories about the danger of being different and of expressing contrary opinions - especially when that divergence brings conflict with those above you in the hierarchy. In order to counter the fears connected with the risk of being different, team diversity and the importance of dissent must be discussed and explored. Team members will only believe that they can speak their own truths boldly and without recrimination when they take the risk to do so and experienced the acceptance of the team and its leader.

This chapter contains thirteen activities that help team members understand not only that expressions of individual opinion are necessary, but it also provides some guidance about how to conduct the conflict of opinion that is embedded in creative collaboration.

Speaking Truth to Power!

Purpose: To make it clear to the team members that diversity of opinion and being willing to disagree with the team leader - and with other team members - is a team expectation.

Equipment: A list of reflective questions as illustrated below.

Process:
- The words of Warren Bennis[1]: *"The first duty of the follower is to speak truth to power"* are written boldly on a white board or easel pad by the team leader.
- The team is divided into 3 or 4 groups (The leader should be in one of the groups). Each group is provided with the same list of reflective questions and given 15 minutes to discuss them before reposting the group's opinions to the whole team.

'Speaking Truth to Power' Reflective Questions:
- What does this phrase really mean?
- Why would team members hesitate to tell the truth (as they see it) to the team leader or school Principal?
- What will happen to the quality of team communication if team members censor their own opinions or hesitate to say anything that may be viewed as different or disloyal?
- Should the manner in which team members disagree be different if the conflict is with the team leader?
- Does this group have any misgivings about reporting their honest opinions to the team and the team leader?

- After every group has reported their opinions the team leader asks:
  o What was common about what we heard from each group?
  o Was anything said that we should discuss as a team?
  o What should be our attitude to internal team conflict in future?
  o How do we manage to disagree between ourselves but unite behind team decisions when they are made?

Reflective Questions: embedded in the activity.

[1].Warren Bennis, *On Becoming a Leader*, 1989.

Exploring the *'I'* in Team

Purpose: To encourage team member appreciation of individual contribution, diversity and autonomy within the framework of the team.

Equipment: A short extract from "The Leader-Mind Equation" (a publication by the author of this book) as it appears on the next page.
A whiteboard or easel pad.

Process:
1. Team members are asked to consider the reading on the next page and make personal notes in the margin about what it means to them.
2. Groups of 2 or 3 are formed and each conducts a PMI analysis (Plus / Minus / Interesting) on the ideas expressed in the text.
3. The ideas from each group are collected and displayed:
4. Team members choose a different group to work with and this time they conduct a 'compass points' analysis (EWNS:
   - Is there anything **E**xciting about this view of team?
   - Is there anything to **W**orry about in the reading?
   - What else do we **N**eed to know in order to be confident about encouraging autonomy in our team?
   - What **S**uggestions do we have for the ways we might foster appreciation of diversity and individual contribution in this team?

Reflective Questions:
- Was the reading a challenge to our usual way of thinking about team?
- What would we gain - or lose - by greater appreciation of the diversity in this team?

The 'I' in Team[1]

"One of the most misleading and thoughtless clichés that pervades the mythology around teams is that 'there is no 'I' in team'!

While this trite phrase draws on a superficial truth about the spelling of TEAM, it misunderstands the reason for having a team. If teams were anonymous components of a collective, simply sublimating their individuality and expertise to an eponymous whole, then this hackneyed phrase would have validity. But this conception of a team is more like a human blancmange than a vigorous collaboration of individuals with their own expertise, opinion and contribution to make.

A real team draws on the disparate talents and personal strength of individuals so that the contribution of each plays a part in the effectiveness of the whole team. The status of a team member has to be far more than an instrument of the collective. When a team's thinking is not allowed to transcend what the team has in common, it limits the potential of the team. Moreover, individuals who would work energetically in a team when their opinions and expertise are appreciated lose interest when they are discouraged from speaking their mind. Team members are most engaged when they can see that the team offers opportunities for success, and for achievements that add to whatever they can attain as individuals.

What this means is that there are many 'I's" in an effective team – as many as there are team members. The team must be designed and managed as a collaboration which harnesses, rather than sublimates, the individual freedom of its members. As the team is formed (and re-formed as its members change) introducing team members to each other in a way that emphasis what is distinctive about each; working in ways that celebrate what each knows and can do - even appreciating the unorthodox - these are the approaches that bring together the individuals in a team to work toward a shared purpose.

A real team has many 'I's. Each of them contributes candidly because they appreciate that what they can do together is greater than whatever they can achieve alone."

[1] *Extract from 'The Leader-Mind Equation' Rob Stones 2020*

The Limits of Diversity

Purpose: To help the team think their way through the proposition that conflict within the team is welcome and healthy but taking the conflict outside the team is damaging. (More on this in the chapter about team decisions).

Equipment: A whiteboard or easel pad to capture the thought of the groups.

Process:

1. Team members are asked to consider these two apparently paradoxical statements:
   - Intra-team conflict is expected - it's built on mutual trust and breeds commitment to team decisions.
   - The willingness of the team to forge collaborative decisions through the flames of diversity, and then to unite behind those decisions, provides the school with certainty and clear direction.
2. Working in small groups team members ask themselves:
   - How do we reconcile the apparent contradictions between the importance of conflict and the unity of team?
   - If we are going to make sense of this paradox as a team, what are the expectations we should have of each other both within team meetings and discussions, and in our communication with the school community?
   - What would be the effects of undermining the decisions of the team outside the team environment?
3. A representative of each of the groups speaks for the group and summarises their opinions on each of the questions. These opinions are captured on the whiteboard.
4. The whole team views the opinions or the groups and discusses any differences. If there is a clear consensus the agreements are added to the team norms or to the values frame of the teams Window of Certainty.
5. If it is clear that there is disagreement or a polarity of views, the team should continue to discuss the issue until a consensus decision can be reached. (See the team decision making chapter for consensus decision-making.)

Note: Many team leaders hesitate to have this discussion for fear that the discussion will be divisive. However, if there is a real difference of opinion it will emerge in team behaviours so it's always better to get this out in the open rather than to leave it to flourish in the dark!

Reflective Questions: Why was it imperative to have that discussion in our team?

Creative Conflict
(how to disagree in an agreeable and productive way!)

Purpose: - To set up the ground rules for dissent and dispute in the team:
- To validate the expression of contrary opinion.
- To set some ground rules for the conduct of disagreement.

Equipment: A large white board (or several wall posters) for part 6 of the activity.

Process:
1. The team leader (or whoever is facilitating the discussion) offers one or more provocative propositions which are certain to elicit disagreement. Examples might be:
   o Being nice to each other is more important that making the best decisions for the school.
   o When people have strong opinions it is natural to be hostile to anyone who disagrees.
   o Because we are so busy it is best for the team to make quick decisions without considering all factors otherwise disagreement may surface.
2. Team members turn to each other and discuss what they think of the propositions offered.
3. They are then asked to work in small groups to consider:
   o Could there ever be a time when those propositions were valid?
   o What would the consequence be if we adopted these propositions as norms?
   o What guidelines can we draw up that would enable us to:
      i. Consider all factors in a decision?
      ii. See every situation from as many perspectives as possible?
      iii. Express strong opinions without hostility and while preserving the trust within the group?
4. Working as a whole team, the members conduct a reverse brainstorm (this will be insightful but also a bit of fun!):
   If we wanted this team to be ineffective and provide really poor leadership for the school, how would we behave in our work together?
   • Now the threads of the 3 parts of the activity are brought together in this way:
   Each Team member in turn suggests a protocol that they think will help the team to:
      • engage in deep reflection and debate;
      • make best-possible decisions;
      • lead the school inspirationally.

5. As each person suggests a protocol the team uses '5-finger voting (see page 100) to respond to their suggestion. If all 5's and 4's (or mostly 5 and 4 plus a small number of 3's) the protocol is adopted and will be written on the Right side of the whiteboard. If the hands reveal a significant degree of doubt because there are many low value votes then the proposed protocol is added to a Problem Paddock on the left side of the board.

6. When all suggestions have been voiced there will be some clearly identified protocols that have been adopted on the right. The team facilitator then asks: Are there and other protocols we should agree to in order to match our 3 criteria from step 5?

7. There is a short open discussion. Suggestions can be taken from the 'Problem Paddock' and re-formulated or new protocols suggested. Any of these become new proposals and are voted in or out using the same method (the hand vote).

8. The team facilitator asks (sometimes several times) can we do any better. Can we improve what we have agreed on? Until the team responds that the protocols agreed are the best that the team can come up with for now, the discussion continues. When all are agreed discussion stops and the protocols on the right side are formally adopted.

Reflective Questions:

- Did we experience disagreement?
- How well did we manage it?
- What could we improve in the way we dealt with different opinions?
- Was this a useful way of achieving consensus in the face of disagreement?
- How could we improve our self-management and communication even further?

Balloon Tai Chi

Purpose: A surprisingly reflective activity. Balloon Tai Chi is a metaphor for the way in which team members can work together in order to achieve harmony while encouraging controlled assertiveness.

Equipment: One balloon for each pair of participants, inflated to a diameter of about 30cm and tied off.

Process:
1. Participants find a partner to work with. Each pair inflates and ties off their balloon.
2. Partners stand facing each other with right foot forward and left foot back – each person's right foot should be alongside that of their partner.
3.

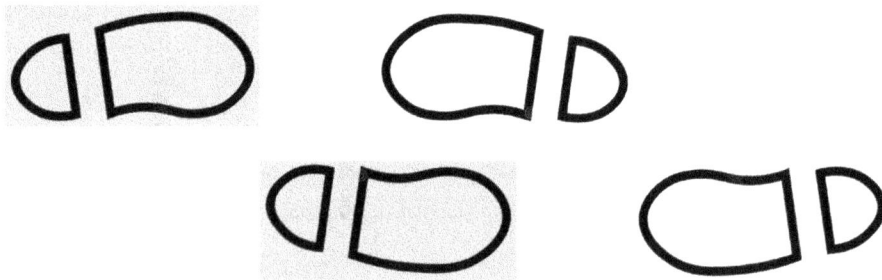

4. Make sure feet are widely enough spaced to form a stable base.
5. Each participant raises their right hand with palm spread and they place the balloon between the palms of their right hand.
6. This instruction is given:
   "Take it in turns to press forward on the balloon while your partner yields and allows their side and shoulder to move back as far as it will comfortably go. When the 'yielding' team member has reached the limits of their flexibility, the person who has been pressing forward will feel the resistance of their partner. At this point, they stop pressing and relax. Now it is the turn of the partner to press forward while the other yields and lets their shoulder and side move backward until the point of natural resistance is reached.
   After you have got the feel of this process, close your eyes and try to establish a rhythmic 'rocking forward and back' process with both of you 'feeling' the amount of tension and relaxation in your partner."

7. When the pairs of participants have experienced this rhythm for a minute or so pause the activity and add this information:

> "I want you to imagine that the balloon symbolises the relationship between team members. To preserve a healthy relationship it is necessary to press forward at times and be honestly and openly assertive. However, that requires the other person to 'give' a bit – to listen and understand. But there is a limit - so as the assertive team member it's important to sense when that limit is reached - and then that's the time for you to switch roles to listening and understanding."

8. Partners continue with the activity for a minute or so thinking about how the balloon represents the relationship and using their senses to gauge when to press forward and when to give.

Team members can change partners if they would like to.

Reflective Questions:

- Why is the balloon a good metaphor for the relationships between team members?
- What can we learn from the metaphor that will help with team cohesion?
- What happens when both press without letting up?
- What else?

Balloon Up

Learned from many sources and demonstrated often by Judy Hatswell - who incorporates it in other processes.

Purpose:

Participants will reflect on the importance of genuine collaboration in order for group goals to supersede individual priorities

Equipment: One balloon per person with as many different colours and patterns as possible.

Process:

1. Participants are each given a balloon. The activity works best if each individual's balloon is of a different shape/pattern to all of the others. Pairs of Balloons can also be used.
2. Participants inflate their balloon to about 30cm diameter.
3. The facilitator gives the instruction: 'The job of the group is to keep all of the balloons in the air, with no balloon touching the ground until the signal that the activity is over is given.'
4. Everyone gathers in the centre of the room and pats their balloon into the air. Once all the balloons are 'up' the job of the group is to work together to keep them up.
5. The facilitator may choose to be a disruptive influence, knocking balloon down towards the ground or out of the reach of participants.
6. The facilitator keeps the activity going past the point where fatigue and confusion set in – constantly urging participants to do better and to keep the balloons off the ground.

Reflective Questions:

- Who attempted to look after their own balloon? Could they?
- Was there a difference between those who stayed in the thick of the action, constantly looking for balloons to keep 'up', and those who stayed on the periphery?
- What was it like for those down on the ground attempting to pick up balloons?
- How is this activity related to the way we work together as a team? Does it have any lessons for us?

Photo Perception

Purpose:

To demonstrate how difficult it is, to fully understand the uniqueness of individual perception. To emphasise the importance of listening and 2nd perceptual position in team communication.

Equipment: A set of photos such as 'Photo-language' or 'Visual Explorer'

Process:

1. Participants are grouped in 3's or 4's. In each group, one person sits out in front of the others and will describe their 'photo'.
2. The facilitator distributes photos to the participants who will describe the photo. The activity works best if the photo set is very varied - if some images are of real objects and if many pictures have an element of ambiguity in their composition.
3. The members of each group attempt to develop as accurate a perception as possible of the picture being described by asking questions of the participant holding the photo.
4. The person holding the photo must answer truthfully.
   a. Closed questions can be answered with a yes or no.
   b. Open questions should be answered fully.
   c. If asked to describe the picture, helpful information should be given.
5. The activity continues until the group believe they have an accurate perception of the photo. They then first describe what they expect to see when the photo is shown to them - **then** they are shown the photo.
6. The activity can be repeated with all having a turn.

Reflective Questions:

- What differences were there between the photo being imagined and the actual photo.?
- How did the knowledge of the 'describer' affect the process?
- What did you learn from this activity about the uniqueness of perception?
- How would the activity be different if the person out at the front was describing how they think about some aspect of our work rather than describing a picture?

The Agenda Wall

Purpose:

To show the importance of having a shared agenda/purpose as a team and the havoc created by personal agendas, especially if they are hidden.

Equipment: 150+ Lego Blocks (or similar) of varying sizes and colours for each group of 3 to 5 participants. 'Personal Agendas' (see below) for every member of each group.

Process:

1. The group task given to every group is to build the most imposing or creative wall possible – the best possible demonstration of the group's ability to create a quality product (or something else suitably vague!)
2. Before building commences, the facilitator issues each participant with their own 'Personal agenda'. Each participant must keep their own agenda secret and try to achieve it.
3. Suggest that there is an element of competition (e.g. "At the end of the activity the final products of each group will be displayed and evaluated").
4. The Facilitator can choose to have NO rules (a free for all) or impose some structure (e.g. 'take turns with each person able to add or remove up to 4 blocks each time they have a turn') Allow 5 to 7 minutes for an initial building phase.
5. Groups MUST work in silence for the initial phase.
6. After the first phase ask the builders to stop. Each person in the group is asked to 'Guess' the agenda of each other group member.
7. After the guesses, each person reveals their actual agenda.
8. The facilitator asks the groups to recommence building, now knowing what the hidden agendas are, but with each person still trying to achieve their own agenda.
9. Halt after another 5 to 7 minutes.
10. Display the products of each group and conduct the de-briefing session.

Reflective Questions:

- What was the effect of the hidden agendas?
- How did you interpret the purpose of other people's hidden agendas?
- What happened when the agendas were public rather that hidden?
- How did even public agendas effect the shared purpose of the group?
- Why were some walls more magnificent (less puny) than others?

Examples of *'Hidden Agendas':*

Note that the facilitator chooses which agendas to give to each group.
Some agendas are very difficult to reconcile, others are more complementary. One group should receive a set of agendas that are comparatively easy to reconcile, others should make an easy resolution almost impossible.

- Your agenda is to ensure that there are three red bricks in each horizontal row.
- Your agenda is to ensure no red brick touches a yellow one.
- Your agenda is to minimise the number of red bricks is the wall.
- Your agenda is to ensure every row contains two yellow bricks.
- Your agenda is to ensure there is a vertical line of touching white bricks, one block wide, from top to bottom.
- Your agenda is to ensure no row contains more than three different-coloured bricks.
- Your agenda is to make sure that the wall is symmetrical.
- Your agenda is to make sure that there are vertical stripes of brick is each row.
- Your agenda is to ensure harmony in the activity of the group.

5 words that Mean....

Purpose: To remind the team about the ambiguity of language. Although we all use words and expressions which may have a relatively clear and precise meaning for ourselves, it's important to remember that these same words and phrases may mean something very different to other team members and colleagues.

Equipment: Pen and paper for everyone.

Process:
1. Write these 5 words on a whiteboard or large sheet of paper:
   - Responsibility; Commitment; Truthfulness; Expertise; Professionalism;
   (You can substitute other words for these to suit the context)
2. Ask every team member to privately write down 5 words or phrases that mean the same as each of the words displayed.
3. When everyone has finished all team members read out exactly what they had written to correspond to each of the 5 words. It's easiest to go around the circle - with each person in turn reading their 5 'same meaning' words or phrases.
4. If a word or phrase has been defined by one person in a way that corresponds exactly to what others have written, those people who have the same definition or meaning raise their hands. That definition or meaning is then not repeated.
5. Emphasise that the match should be reasonable exact – not 'something like'.
6. One person in the team keeps a tally of how many people raised their hands (i.e. had the same definition or meaning for) each of the 5 words.
7. After all meanings have been read the tally – the number of identical meanings/definitions – is noted against each of the 5 words. The numbers will be surprisingly small!

Reflective Questions:
- Were we surprised by the result?
- What inferences can we draw?
- What generalisations can we make?

In his book 'The Advantage' Patrick Lencioni urges teams to 'Create Clarity' then 'Overcommunicate Clarity' then 'Reinforce Clarity'. How is that relevant to this exercise?

TOWERS

Purpose: To demonstrate how easily team members can default to competitive mode unless there is a clear purpose and rationale for working together.

Equipment: any materials such as building blocks, cards, coins, counters, books, paper and tape ... you must have a copious supply of whatever you choose.

Process: Arm each individual with the chosen equipment and ask them to build the tallest tower possible from the material provided.

After several minutes the emerging competition between individuals will become obvious even though there was no hint in the instruction that the activity was competitive.

Reflective Questions 1:
- Ask participants how they came to the conclusion that it was a competition: discuss the way that they formed that perception.

Re-start the activity: This time, ask the participants how much more successful they can be if they encouraged to work collaboratively, working in groups to build one tower for each group.

Usually, the towers will be higher than those previously constructed - but it is quite usual for competition between groups to emerge at this stage.

Reflective Questions 2:
- In what ways was collaboration more successful than competition?
- Why and how did competition emerge between groups?
- Which of the Human needs (Achievement / Status, Freedom/Autonomy, Survival, Fun and Learning, Relationships / Connectedness) is explained by, and which threatened by, competition?
- In what way do our conclusions apply to our work together as a team?

Railway Carriages

Purpose: To elicit honest opinion or feedback from group members in such a way that it is delivered anonymously.

Equipment: A chair for each participant. The chairs are placed in two rows, facing each other with about 60cm between the rows and chairs in each row almost touching each other. E.g.:

Each participant has a note pad and pen.

Process:

1. Identify the issue about which feedback or opinion is sought and frame two questions to be asked: one question should be framed positively and one framed negatively. (E.g.: 'What's the best way for the team to be more effective' / 'What is the reason we are not being effective at present').
2. Nominate one row as row A, the other as Row B
3. A's job is to ask the positive form of the question, B's ask the question in the negative.
4. When the facilitator says GO, A's addresses their question to B. B's respond to the question and A's write down B's response. In this way the person answering the question always has what they said recorded by the person opposite.
5. After 45 seconds (can be a minute) the facilitator calls STOP.
6. A's move one place to the right, (B's stay where they are) the end A moves to the other end.
7. When all have moved, the facilitator asks B's to GO and they ask their question and write down the answers they hear.
8. Again after 45 seconds the facilitator call STOP and this time B's move one place to their right.
9. Continue this process for at least 4 to 5 exchanges from each side. The facilitator can change the negative/positive form of the question so that it is asked by the other side at any time.

10. The entire group then shares what they heard by simply reading out what they have written on their note pad. Of course, this is always what another person said, so its source is anonymous. If the group is large, they can be grouped to hear the feedback.

Reflective Questions:

The facilitator leads a debrief of the activity along the lines of:

- What did we hear?
- What did we learn?
- Were there some clear messages heard?
- Are there some suggested actions or next steps as a result of what we have learned?

Optimising Team Performance

Based on Patrick Lencioni's work: '*The 5 Dysfunctions of Team*'.

Purpose: To explore the difference between dysfunctional and effective teams. To draw conclusions about the nature and origins of team dysfunction and work out how to avoid it.

Process:

1. The first part of the process is based on 3 questions which team members answer in groups. If the team is small the whole team can discuss the questions. If the team is large, then smaller groups will be better.

    I.   An important decision has to be made by the team, but team members are discouraged from expressing their opinions freely and many don't agree with the decision made. How committed to the decision and resulting course of action will be the team members who did not agree and could not voice their views?

    II. To what extent will team members feel accountable for and work hard for the success of a decision in which they could not fully participate and with which they do not agree?

    III. How likely is at that these team members will attend to and care about whether the actions that flow from the decision have a successful result?

2. In '*The 5 dysfunctions of team*' Lencioni suggests that unwillingness to embrace and engage with healthy conflict is the result of at least one of these conditions:

    a. The team has not reached a level of vulnerability-based trust that allows team members to be open and honest with each other.

    b. Team members don't trust each other enough to recognise and rely on each other's strengths and find it difficult to acknowledge their own imperfections.

    c. The team leader is reluctant to allow conflict from fear that he or she may lose 'control' of team process and interaction.

    d. Both team members and the team leader prefer to cut meetings and discussions short and rush to a decision to save time

    - Which, if any, of these conditions might exist in this team?
    - Are we willing to talk about it?

3. Step 3 in this process is for team members to engage with and discuss these 5 features of optimal team performance:

    FIRST and most important create a cohesive and functional team through establishing a solid foundation of vulnerability-based trust. This means that members must be willing to learn to comfortably and readily accept that they don't have all the answers and may need the support and assistance of the tea. It's also important to recognize and respect the strengths of others, even when those strengths exceed their own.

Secondly. Adopt the practice of making the best use of the team by encouraging diverse opinions, healthy conflict and the importance of making good decisions and implementing strong leadership in ways that draw on the contributions of all team members.

THIRDLY: Agree to commit to the best decisions the team can make, and which are aligned with the team's purpose. Even when absolute consensus does not emerge, the team's job is to remain focused on purpose. Because perfect insight and completely natural consensus rarely exist, the ability to commit becomes one of the most critical behaviours of a team.

Fourth: Hold each other accountable. Because the debate within the team has been rigorous enough, and the decision clear enough team members will be certain about what they have committed to do. They must be willing to identify and call each other on actions and behaviours that don't contribute to the likelihood of success.

Fifth: Attend to the outcomes that the team is working toward as your priority. As a team member this is the only real scorecard for measuring its success. And while the team may include individual leaders who are driven to succeed personally, that should never interfere with the pursuit of team outcomes.

Reflective Questions
- How has this discussion been important for our team?
- What did you notice that validates the way that we are already going about our work as a team?
- Are there some aspects of the way this team functions that we should pay more attention to and improve?
- As individuals, are there some things that we will change or commit to in future?

The Meta-Mirror

Purpose: To enable team members to view any situation or problem from multiple perspectives. This activity is particularly useful when the team is in the process of making a decision which will have ramifications for others across the school community.

Equipment: The numbers 1 – 4 arranged as shown in the diagram below.

Process: Set out the 4 numbers as shown.

1. Each of the numbers represent one of the perceptual positions (refer to the team formation chapter) – the four different ways of paying attention.

2. The 4 perceptual positions will be 'walked' either by one representative of the team or by the whole team if the activity is conducted in a large space.

3. Start at first position: how does this situation currently look from the perspective of this team?

4. Then walk to 2nd position. How does the same situation appear from the point of view of those most affected (probably teachers or students)?

5. Move to 3rd position. If we were impartial observers, how would we describe the situation objectively? Make sure that the words used are non-judgmental. Can the team think of a metaphor that describes the situation?

6. Move to 4th Position. This is the big picture: the good of the school in the future – the perspective of history! The team might want to ask themselves what they would like to say about the decision they will make if they were speaking proudly about it 5 years in the future?

7. Now move back to 1st position and ask: has anything changed as a result of that activity? Have we changed anything about the way we see this problem?

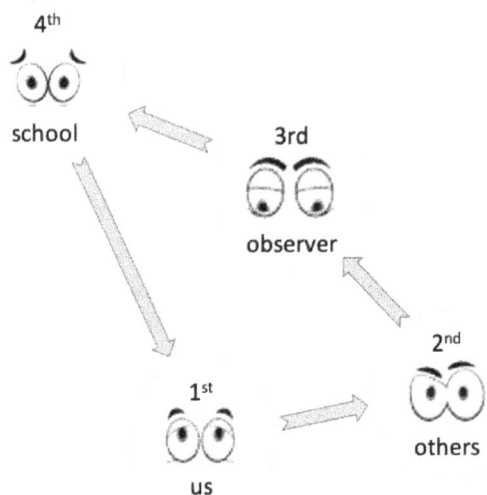

Reflective Questions
- What difference did it make to be quite deliberate about taking different positions and paying attention to the situation in different ways?
- Which position was most interesting or added a new viewpoint to the situation?

Section Four

Team Purpose and Expectation

Of all of the activities and conversations conducted within a team, these are the most important:

- Deciding on the Team's Purpose;
- Setting expectations about the team's role in the school;
- Establishing and clarifying the ways that team members work together.

These conversations are vital because when any group of people is working together, they must know *where they are going*, *why they need each other,* and *how they will collaborate*. These three practices are central to the effectiveness of all the teams in the school. It does not matter if it is the Executive Team, a Faculty or Stage Team, a Project team or the team of the whole staff: clarity of purpose, mutual expectations and productive ways of working together are always crucial.

In this chapter these three priorities are addressed in several different ways through the sixteen activities.

The Window of Certainty© is a recommended strategy for pulling together vision and purpose, outcomes, beliefs and values in a way that will provide autonomy for team members - whilst drawing important boundaries around their team responsibilities. The processes for 'visioning', 'purpose', 'outcomes', 'making agreement visible' and 'refining consensus' can all be used in creating the Window of Certainty. Alternatively, they can be used as stand-alone processes for setting direction and achieving cohesion.

Other activities in this chapter help team members to clarify the nature of their role, explore the limits of leadership and discuss the behaviours that are most likely to help them become increasingly influential.

Some of the activities in this chapter require thoughtful preparation and can be quite hard work compared to other activities in the book. They will be worth the effort!

'The Window of Certainty'©

Purpose:

The 'Window of Certainty'© is a powerful instrument for setting team purpose and clear direction. It consists of 4 Frames that define the zone within which the team can work with energy and confidence.

The frames of the Window delineate the boundaries within which team members agree to work. Within these boundaries, individual team members can and should exploit their personal autonomy and style.

As well as creating team cohesion the activity of defining the team's 'Window of Certainty' is a rich source of productive professional conversation.

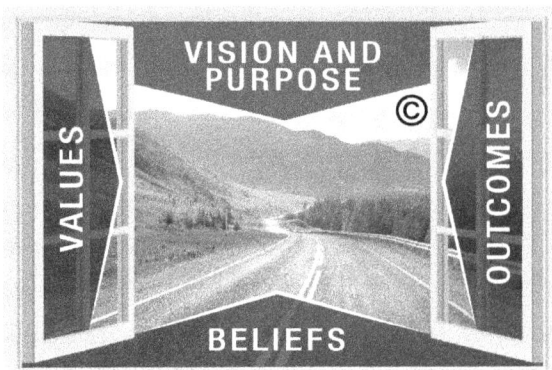

Equipment: Large easel pads or A3 paper, Pens. Post-it notes and 'sticker dots may be useful. (Note: more detailed processes for creating the frames of the 'Window of Certainty' can be found in the following pages)

Process:

Put aside time to create the Window. It is essential that 'the window' is a co-creation of the team - consequently it will take hours rather than minutes to construct. The resulting range and depth of the conversations may take time but will be rewarded by optimal team clarity and certainty.

Create the four frames of the 'Window' in this order:

1. The Vision Frame. Every team needs a statement of aspirational intent. The key is the question: "Where are we going?" The team first defines its destination – a realistic but stretch goal for the future. In the school setting the team's purpose will always be focused on optimising student success and well-being.

2. The Outcomes Frame is created from the team's response to the questions: "What will success look like?" and "How will we measure our progress?" Defining the outcomes that will eventuate if the team achieves its purpose allows the team to measure progress and stay on task.

3. The Beliefs Frame provides strategic impetus to the team's purpose. Beliefs are our trusted perceptions of how success is achieved – in this case the perceptions of what will be effective and how will the team must work together to achieve its outcomes. The Question to be addressed are: "What do we believe will have to happen in this team for our outcomes to be achieved?". This frame requires some deep conversation and the focus must be on making sure that the beliefs the team adopts are aligned with each other. Contradictory beliefs create confusion at the strategic level. However, when beliefs are aligned then team cohesion and strategic unity are promoted.

4. The Values Frame helps the team to design and encourage the culture in which they will work together. The accent is on 'values in action' rather than simply abstract value statements. The question to be addressed here is: "What values should underpin the way we work with, support, and interact with each other?" The values frame helps the team to identify the ethical principles that will unite them and details what these mean in practice.

More details about the kind of processes which can be used to collaboratively develop the frames are included in the following pages of this section.

For a full description and a detailed 'technical manual' for creating the Window of Certainty you can purchase the paperback or e-book: "The Window of Certainty" by Rob Stones and Judy Hatswell at www.futureshape.com.au

Reflection and Follow-Up Questions

There will be many opportunities to use the Window of Certainty after it has been created. Every time a new change is proposed, a decision must be made or there are alternative courses of action for the team to follow then the Window becomes a reference point. Question such as these help to maintain team alignment and the pursuit of shared purpose:

- How does this help us achieve our vision and purpose?
- What will lead us most effectively to the outcomes we have identified?
- Do these proposed strategies match our shared beliefs?
- In what way will these actions promote the values we have adopted?

Visioning: Dreaming the Future

(Can be used to create the Vision Frame of the 'Window of Certainty'©
or as a stand-alone activity)

Purpose: Jean Paul Sartre defined imagining as: "the ability to see what is not."
Creating the vision for a team is exactly that sort of activity. It prompts the team to see
beyond the present reality and imagine a desired future. It's important that the vision
seems attainable – but just beyond the present reach of the team.

Equipment: A blank page and pen for each team member.

Process: Eliciting the vision is a two-step process:

> Step 1: create questions that encourage the imagination to fly.
> Step 2: ground the imagined future to an attainable level.

Without the second step the dreaming can easily become fantasy!

Step 1:

a) Split the team into 4 groups and ask each group a different question. The following are
examples (you may think of even better ones):

> Q1 – What newspaper headlines about our school would you love to see appear in the
> next few years and which will have resulted from the efforts of this team?
> Q2 – When you consider your personal ambitions as a teacher and a leader, what kind
> of achievements would you be proud of?
> Q3 – imagine that you were given the opportunity to talk to a room full of parents
> who are considering our school for their child. What is it that you would like to be
> able to say to them?
> Q4 – If we knew we could not fail, what would we try to achieve for our school and
> our students?

b) Group members sit in a circle. For 10 minutes, each person in the group writes their
own answers to the question.

c) After 10 minutes, everyone passes their contribution to the team member on their left.
Allow 3 minutes for them to read and write comments.

d) Continue passing the contributions every 3 minutes.

e) When each participant has seen every contribution and read the comments on their
own the group discusses what they wrote or read that excited them and what they
would like to see captured in some way in the vision. They should not be too concerned
with actual wording at this point – this is the pure dreaming stage.

f) Each group agrees between two and four key ideas they would like to see carried forward into the agreed vision statement.

Step 2:
I.   Each group reports on the 2-4 ideas they would like adopted into the vision statement. Each of the other groups choose one of these ideas to analyse, audit and refine. Every group will end up working on ideas for the vision that were initiated by another group.

II.   Note: ideas from the groups in Step 1 may be remarkably similar, so in Step 2 the groups may choose to work on 'like ideas'.

III. As groups work on the contributions to the vision statement their aim is to sharpen and clarify the original.

IV.   As the groups develop refined versions of the vision statement, they then check with the group who initiated the idea to make sure that their interpretation still retains the intention of the original.

V.   All the refined ideas are displayed for the whole team. Either the whole team, or a specialist writing group nominated by the team, will now synthesise the disparate contributions into one statement of vision. This may take some time.

When the synthesised vision statement is completed it is presented to the group who may:
- Accept it – it becomes the team's vision statement;
- Want it further modified – continue to work on it by refining the language, adding what is missing or cutting anything that is unnecessary until a statement that is acceptable to the whole group is completed.

Questions for reflection:
- Is this a vision we can all aspire to?
- Do we all agree that it is attainable if we work together effectively?

The Vision statement (and the intended outcomes that flow from it) will be used to focus discussion and decision-making at most team meetings.

Defining _Team_ Purpose

Purpose: To create a clear and concise team purpose statement that can help focus the collaborative efforts of all team members. A statement of the explicit purpose of the team itself (different from - but aligned with - the Vision and Purpose of the School) is often helpful!

Equipment: Paper and pens

Process:
1. Divide the team into smaller groups of 2 to 4 (depending on the size of your team).
2. When the small groups have been established, explain that you want each small group to create what they feel is a team purpose statement that they can make reference to in order to be highly motivated and outcome focused.
3. The team purpose statement should not exceed 2-3 concise sentences.
4. the following questions can be considered by the groups when they are drafting their purpose statement:
   - What contribution do we make to the school that no one else can make?
   - Where are we going as a team to help us feel we are making progress?
   - What is the most important thing for our team to be recognised for?
   - What is the special contribution we can make to the school?
   - What do we need to depend on each other for?
   - What do we want to be seen and respected for? - By colleagues; Parents; Students; Senior Executives.
5. A writing group collates the contributions of the small groups into one statement of purpose for the whole team and presents it for editing and approval at the next meeting.
   OR Use the process suggested in Step 2 on the previous page.

Reflective Questions:
- Is the purpose for our executive team, stage team or faculty team tightly focused on the importance of our work?
- Does our statement of purpose help us to be clear about our contribution to the school?

Outcomes

Purpose: To ensure that the vision is sharpened and refined sufficiently to provide clear and unambiguous goals for the team to work towards. There are times when this process leads to a further refinement of the vision itself.

Equipment: A copy of the Vision or purpose statement the team has created. Writing materials. Card size post-it notes are often useful.

Process:

1. Every element of the Team's Vision or Statement of Purpose is separated out.
2. Team members work in pairs and ask themselves:
- What will be the observable indicators that we are making progress toward this element of the vision, or have achieved our intended purpose? (Observable indicators may be numerical data, results of opinion surveys, feedback from significant sources or even anecdotal data that has at least face validity).
3. As teach pair identifies outcomes that they believe are appropriate they post them on an easel pad or whiteboard.
4. As each contribution is posted, those outcome statements that have been previously displayed are scrutinized carefully and the new contribution is grouped with any that are similar.
5. When all the outcome statements have been added and grouped, small groups are formed to consider each group of outcome expressions. They use the SMART formula to scrutinize the statement they are working on and try to create an articulation of each outcome which is:
    i. **Specific;**
    ii. Clearly **Measurable** or assessable;
    iii. **Attractively** framed as inspiration for the team;
    iv. Appears **Realistic** and attainable;
    v. Is expressed with a defined **time frame**.
6. The resulting outcome statements are published as widely as possible and refined as a result of any feedback received.

Reflective Questions:
- If we achieve these outcomes will we have achieved our vision and purpose?
- Is there any part of our team vision which is not captured in our outcomes?

Making Agreement Visible

Purpose: To canvas the range of belief within the team and then identify the areas of agreement. This activity can be used to construct the beliefs frame of the Window of Certainty - in which case the aim will be to identify the beliefs of the group about what will enable the team to achieve its identified outcomes.

Equipment: 6 x 6cm 'post it' notes and pens. Large easel pads or similar on which to stick the 'post-it' notes.

Process:
1. The sphere in which beliefs should be expressed should first be discussed so that everyone is clear about expectations: E.g. 'these are our beliefs about the ways we will achieve our stated outcomes'.
2. Individuals write their own opinions, values or beliefs on 'Post-it' notes - one thought or viewpoint on each note.
3. When everyone has had a chance to make their individual contribution, team members pair off and identify areas of agreement. The best expression of that agreement should be conserved for the next stage.

> Note that agreements should not be contrived or approximated. Vigorous debate and diversity of thought should be encouraged.

4. Each pair teams up with another pair and the same process is followed.
5. If the team is large, this process continues until the team is working in groups of 8.
6. The products of each group discussion are then posted on easel pads or 'butchers' paper. Similar ideas are grouped and then the main threads of agreement are identified through the volume of similar ideas.
7. If there are too many different beliefs, 'sticker dots' (next page) can be used to refine the most compelling areas of agreement.
8. Small groups work on the best way to express all of the areas of apparent agreement and these are published as the consensus of the group.
9. Time is allowed for these to be reviewed and further discussed until it is agreed that consensus has been achieved.

Reflective Questions:
- Have we captured all of the main threads of agreement?
- Is there some polarity of beliefs that we will need to work through as a team?
- Is any belief or opinion marginalised by this process?

Refining Consensus with 'Sticker-Dots'

Purpose: To visually identify areas of clear agreement and enhance progress towards consensus. Often a team has trouble identifying the difference between the most passionate voices and the consensus of opinion – this process helps to make visible the most generally held beliefs and opinions

Equipment: A display of the varied opinions or beliefs of the group on any issue.
Seven to ten sticker dots for each person.

Process:
1. Group all of the varied opinions. If these are known from previous activity put them on display. If starting from scratch, use a process such as 'Making Agreement Visible' using 'Post-It Notes' (previous page).
2. Every team member has 7 to 10 sticker dots that they can use to identify the beliefs and ideas that they strongly agree with - or think will be most effective. They place one dot on each idea they support. Participants do not have to use all their dots.
3. It will immediately be visibly obvious which opinions or ideas have the clear support of the group. Circle these with a marker to identify them.
4. It will be clear which of the ideas are not well supported (only one or two dots). Remove these.
5. There will be some ideas that have a moderate level of support. Allow one advocate of each of these ideas one minute to speak in favour.
6. Give team members 3 more dots of a different colour which they can (if they wish) allocate to one of the moderately supported ideas for which have just heard advocacy.
7. If any of these ideas have now garnered strong support, they are circled and added to the consensus list.

Reflective Questions:
- Are we satisfied that the ideas / beliefs / values identified represent the consensus view of the group?
- Are we all prepared to commit to these?
- Under what circumstances should we revisit these?

Conversational Mapping

Making Sense of Complex Situations.

Purpose: To bring a sense of order and clarity to complex situations when there is a lot going on and the team needs to identify the 'parts' of the problem in order to understand the competing forces and priorities involved.

Equipment: Easel pads or A2 paper, many different-coloured pens.

Process:
1. Conversational Mapping: working in groups of 3 to 4 team members (fewer if your team is small) discuss as many aspects of the complexity facing them as they can think of. This might seem a bit overwhelming but reassure them that their job is just to identify all the strands of the situation in order to identify them. Each team member notes down the aspects of the situation that are most important or most troubling for them.
   There is no need for agreement so everyone may have noted different things.
2. After 10 minutes or so the groups create a 'brain dump map'. Remaining in their small group, each group simply dumps (writes down) all of their own notes on the same large sheet of paper. In the middle of the paper write a couple of words to describe the complex situation and then all around this team members write their notes in separate clusters of thought. New aspects of the situation may come up as this is being done and it's OK to jot those down as well.
3. The next step is to track these conversational notes with mind-webs. Simply look for connections between all of the different thoughts, fears, ideas and insights that have been written down - then connect these with a line between them.

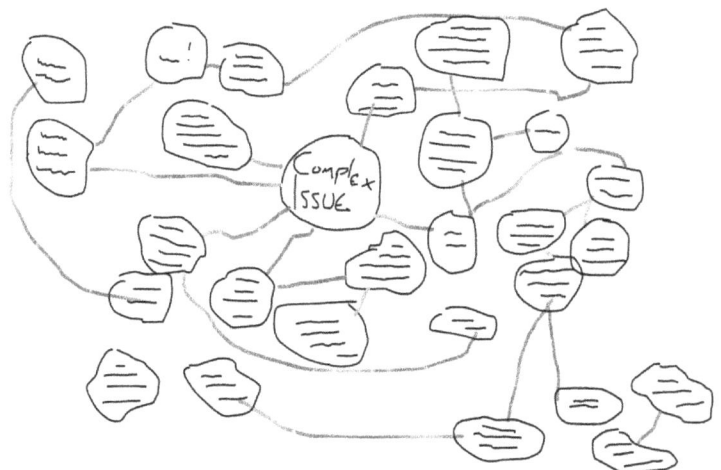

4. Now add some graffiti that gives the connected ideas 'names' such as 'staff reactions' or 'decisions that need to be made' or 'situations to avoid'. When completed all of the mind-webs are

posted around the room for the whole team to view. Team members from other groups may ask questions to clarify the connections and names on the mind web's created by other groups.

5. Working as a whole team, the team members are now in a position to identify the major themes (the ones that appeared in most webs) and the minor but connected themes. It will probably become obvious that some notes are not related to the main complex issue so put those aside to be dealt with separately.

6. Once the main themes have been identified, tease out and discuss the underlying beliefs and assumptions from these themes. These should be discussed and may be challenged. Where do these beliefs stand against our team purpose or our 'Window of Certainty'? (The team should always be conscious of aligning with the vision, outcomes, beliefs and values they have previously created.)

7. Now the team has identified the major areas to be dealt with, and identified the key beliefs and assumptions involved the paths to action become clearer. Some courses of action will be obvious. For others the team may need to develop action plans. The 'Rational Change Model' (which can be found on pages 110-111of this book) can be useful for this.

Reflective Questions:
- Have we identified the main themes of this complex situation, and the associated beliefs and assumptions?
- Did this process enable us to stand back from the complexity and see where everything stood in the light of our established vision and beliefs?

The Fist

Purpose: To illustrate an important principle of team interaction and leadership: people automatically respond to being compelled in a predictably oppositional manner. It's in our genes - *when we are pushed, we push back!*

Process:

1. Pair off and stand in 2 lines, with partners facing each other.
2. The team members in one line extend their arm with fist clenched and try not to move their fist, whatever the other person does.
3. The team members on the other hand push against their partner's fist with their own clenched fist.
4. Team members discover that the harder they are pushed, the harder they push back!
5. Change over and have the other side become the pushers.
6. Now illustrate that gentle persuasion is far more productive than pressure. Have the team members in the first line again hold out their fist (arm extended). Once again give the instruction to try not to move the fist.
7. This time their partner does not push, but very gently - using just a couple of fingers - moves the other person's fist up or down or side to side. The person with their arm extended may try to resist but will find that even when they are trying really hard their fist can be easily moved.
8. Change over again so that everyone experiences this.

Reflective Questions:

- What did this activity illustrate about how we should work with each other and our colleagues, students and other members of the school community?
- What does it imply about the importance of the levels of openness and honesty that we have committed to as a team?

Chairs

Purpose:
Participants will see that apparently conflicting goals can be resolved if communication is
  clear and issues are discussed.

Equipment: Sufficient chairs (one per participant). 4 different group instruction slips.

Process:
1. Participants are divided into 4 groups. Each group is given a slip of paper on which are
   written instructions about how to arrange the chairs in the room:
   a) Group 1: Arrange the chairs in a circle around the room.

   b) Group 2: Arrange the chairs so that they are stacked in pairs.

   c) Group 3: Arrange the chairs so that they are overturned.

   d) Group 1: Arrange the chairs so that they face outwards.

Groups can discuss their own instruction slip quietly but do not share with other groups.

2. Give the signal GO and allow 2 minutes for the groups to 'compete' against each other.

3. Then STOP the activity and ask groups to share the instructions they were given.

4. Allow 3 minutes for discussion about how the apparently different instructions can be
   reconciled.

5. Allow 2 more minutes for the participants to complete the activity.

Reflective Questions:
• What did you learn from this activity?
• What did the activity demonstrate about reconciling apparently different agendas?
• How might you use the principles derived from this activity to enhance team
  effectiveness?

Community Juggling

Purpose:
    a. To demonstrate that people coordinate their activities best if there is a system - and everyone is clear about what to do.
    b. To show that there is always a limit to how much the team can take on.

Equipment: Juggling balls. Comfortable group size is less than 20 – probably about 12-14 preferred. 1 ball per person.

Process:
1. Group members are asked to throw the balls back and forward to each other across the circle and to keep all the balls moving as fast as possible. Use only two-thirds of the balls. Chaos usually ensues in a short time!
2. The facilitator then helps the group to create a system. This time participants gently lob the ball to the person on their left and keep all balls going around the circle. Balls must leave the hand, not be passed.
3. When the system is established ask everyone to notice who they receive balls from and who they pass the ball to.
4. Now ask <u>every second</u> participant to move to the other side of the circle from where they have been standing.
5. Resume the activity with each person always receiving the ball from the same person and giving to the same person as in steps 2 and 3.
6. The facilitator can coach the group by emphasising:
   - Good service (accuracy of passing).
   - Eye contact (good communication).
7. When the balls are effectively whizzing around the group keep adding more balls.

Reflective Questions.
- What worked to improve the predictability and effectiveness of the process?
- How does this create an effective metaphor for collaborative teamwork?
- What happened when more and more balls were introduced?
- How can we apply our insights from this to the way our team can work together?
- Is there a limit to what the team can do?

Which of our Roles is MOST Important?

Purpose: To help team members consider and choose their roles in the school. All of the activities listed in the table may be regarded as appropriate conduct for team members in a school. The aim of this exercise is to help team members to discriminate between the potential roles associated with their positions and decide which are the most important.

Equipment: The 'What is our role?' table for each person.

Process:
1. The critical choice for the leader is to decide which activities define them, and which role(s) are central to their contribution to the school.
2. The actions associated with the three views of executive roles are derived from writing by Peter F. Drucker:

What is our role?

Leaders	Managers	Administrators
Do the right thing.	Do things right.	Do the next thing.
Find a way forward.	Follow the rules.	Tidy up.
Engage with complexity.	Keep things simple.	Ensure consistency.
Provide Inspirational vision.	Create efficient processes.	Devise procedural systems.
Influence people.	Manage people.	Assigns tasks to people.
Ask Why? and What if?	Asks How? and When?	Tell people what to do.
Have long-term perspective.	Adopt short-term perspective.	Adopt a task perspective.
Create the future.	Manage the present.	Organize events.

3. Team members work individually to circle the activities that seem to occupy most of their time.
4. They then work in pairs to consider which of the activities will be likely to make most difference to the students and achieve optimal outcome for every student in the school. They underline the actions that they believe will make the most difference or will enhance the performance of the school and its students.
5. The table is posted and each pair circles and underlines whatever they chose.
6. The whole group discusses what they believe this shows about their orientation and priorities as a team.

Reflective Questions: What does this exercise show about where we should direct our energy? Are there some changes in focus we should make?

What are we meeting for?

Purpose: - For the team to consider the purpose of team meetings.
- To provide ways to identify the purpose of specific items in a meeting agenda.

Equipment: This page can be printed as a 'worksheet' for each team member

Process:

A. The team works in pairs to hear and respond to a series of provocative propositions:
   1. The reason for our meetings is mainly to receive accurate information that we can pass on to the other people that we work with;
   2. Our principal job as a team is to solve problems as they arise and react to emergent difficulties;
   3. We don't have time to keep revisiting our strategic purpose and progress towards outcomes in our meetings;
   4. We know all we need to know about leading the school so there is little point in spending time learning how to work together and improve our leadership;
   5. All meetings should be decision-making meetings in which the team makes decisions about present and future options;
   6. Detailed planning is impossible in education because there is so much change that we can't control - so there is no point in making plans in our meetings;
   7. As mature professionals we should be responsible for our own review and reflection so it's not necessary to spend reflection and review time in our meetings;
   8. All meetings are a waste of time so we should each get on with our individual jobs.

B. If our team meetings were spent on 'just the right of time' spent on each of the following:
   - i. Hearing information
   - ii. Solving problems
   - iii. Reviewing our strategic process
   - iv. Learning more about leadership and teamwork.
   - v. Making decisions
   - vi. Planning
   - vii. Reflecting on and reviewing our performance;

   What would the right amount of time look like to you as an individual?

C. The numbers 1 to 7 are written on the whiteboard and each team member puts a %age that represents the 'right amount of time' next to each of the team functions.

Reflective Questions: - What do we need to clarify about the purpose of our team?
- How much diversity is there in our ideas about what team meeting should be for?
- Do we need variety of processes and practices in order to cater for everyone?
- Are there some changes in emphasis that we ought to consider for future meetings?

What Leadership Means to Me?

A Visual Explorer Activity.

Purpose: For team members to clarify the meaning and purpose of their leadership role in the school and to discuss how their leadership as a team will be developed.

Equipment: A set of '*Visual Explorer*' cards from the Centre for Creative Leadership (USA) or similar sets such as '*photolanguage*' from the Catholic Education Office, Sydney or other picture resources available from St Luke's Innovative Resources in Bendigo.

Process:
1. The Leadership Explorer Cards are spread out on the floor or on tables.
2. Team members are asked to choose between 2 and 4 images that illustrate some aspect of what leadership means to them.
3. The team sits in a circle and each takes a turn to show the photos they have chosen and what the photos mean to them about leadership. The photos chosen are laid in the centre of the circle where they are clearly visible to everyone.
4. When everyone has shared their photos and described what they mean, the team breaks up into groups of 3. Each group talks about the ways in which team members view leadership and identifies the images and associated meanings that resonate with them.
5. As a small group they choose 3 photos and their meanings to promote to the whole team.
6. The whole team reconvenes, groups share their preferred 3 images and meanings and tries to identify common themes.

Reflective Questions:
- What did that activity tell us about the diversity or the consistency of our views about leadership?
- Do we seem to share a consensus about some aspects of leadership?
- Are there some features of our differences in thinking that we should discuss further to see if we can achieve greater consistency in our expectations and assumptions?

Note: Within a stage team or faculty team the discussion might be reframed as 'What the Leadership of Students means to me' or 'What Teaching means to me'.

Connecting and Disconnecting

Based on the work of Dr. William Glasser MD.

Purpose: for team members to explicitly identify and discuss the behaviours that help them connect (to each other, to their team members and to students and parents) and those that are disconnecting.

Equipment: Paper and Pens, plus copies of the 'Connecting and Disconnecting Behaviours' from the next page.

Process:

1. Team members initially work on their own.
2. Each person I asked to write down a list of the behaviours used by other people which they experience as connecting - i.e. those which increase rapport and trust between them.
3. After 5 minutes, they are asked to write a separate list of those behaviours they experience as disconnecting – i.e. those that damage trust and liking and harm the relationship.
4. After a further 5 minutes, team members pair off with another person and they compare their two sets of lists. They put a check against all of the connecting and all of the disconnecting behaviours upon which they agree.
5. The List on the next page, based on connecting and disconnecting behaviours as identified by Dr. William Glasser is distributed to the team. As a whole team they discuss which (if any) behaviours they can add to Dr. Glasser's list and whether there are any behaviours on the Glasser list that they don't agree with.
6. The team should finish with an agreed list of connecting and disconnecting behaviours.

Reflective Questions:

- In what circumstances - and with whom - do we use disconnecting behaviours?
- Are disconnecting behaviours ever successful? - or are they usually behaviours that we choose because we don't know what else to do?
- Who are the people with whom we usually take care to use connecting behaviours?
- What are the implications of these lists for the way that we encourage our own effectiveness as a team?

Connecting and Disconnecting

Based on lists developed by Dr. William Glasser MD.

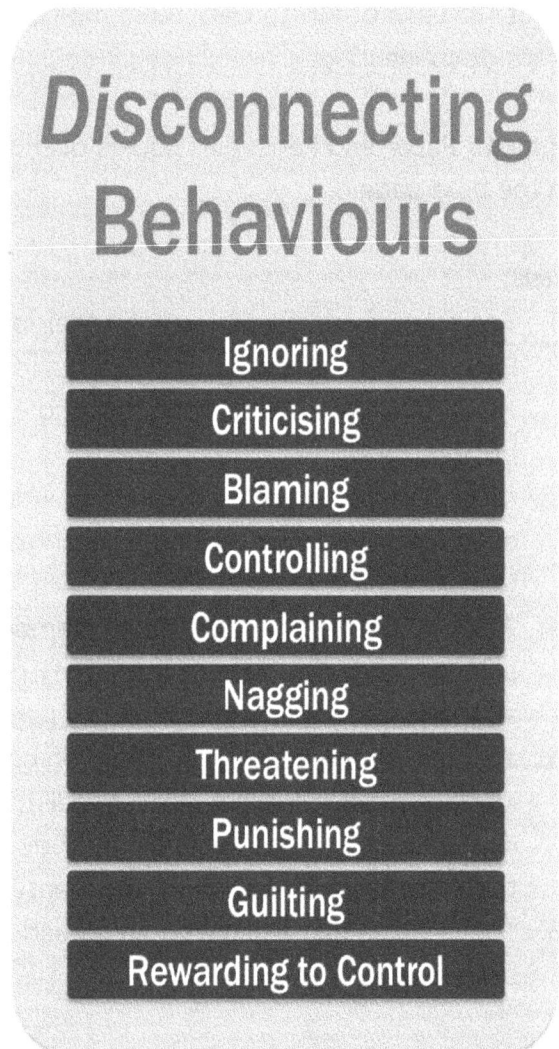

Connecting Behaviours	Disconnecting Behaviours
Caring	Ignoring
Listening	Criticising
Supporting	Blaming
Contributing	Controlling
Encouraging	Complaining
Trusting	Nagging
Befriending	Threatening
Negotiating	Punishing
Respecting Differences	Guilting
	Rewarding to Control

Above or Below the Green Line

Based on concepts developed by Margaret Wheatley and explained by Phil Boas.

Purpose: To create open discussion about the culture of the school or team by using Margaret Wheatley's model as a discussion starter.

Equipment: A copy for each team members of the 'Above and Below the Green Line' model which is on the next page

Process:

1. The 'Above and Below the Green Line' model, based on the work of Margaret Wheatley is presented.
2. The team member facilitating the discussion explains that there is a balance needed. A school that works mostly above the green line will be efficient, but the staff and students may not be energised and enthusiastic. Conversely, a school that is working almost solely below the green line might be relational and energetic - but may also be uncertain or chaotic.
3. Team members work in pairs identifying the parts of the model that they can relate to how the school (or their team within the school) is presently operating. They make a note of features of the school culture that are important and of those that they would like to discuss or possibly change.
4. A whole team discussion focuses on the questions: 'have we got the balance right?' and: 'Are there some areas where we should focus differently either above or below the line?'

Reflective Questions:

- Does the 'Above and Below the Green Line' model give us a useful way of analyzing our culture?
- Have we identified some aspects of culture that we would like to change?
- Are relying too much on either "above the line' or 'below the line' practices?
- Does the model give us some indicators that we can use when morale is low or when there is lack of certainty and direction in our school or team?

Wheatley – Above and Below the Green Line

Based on the 6 Circle Model developed by Margaret Wheatley and Tim Dalmau 1983

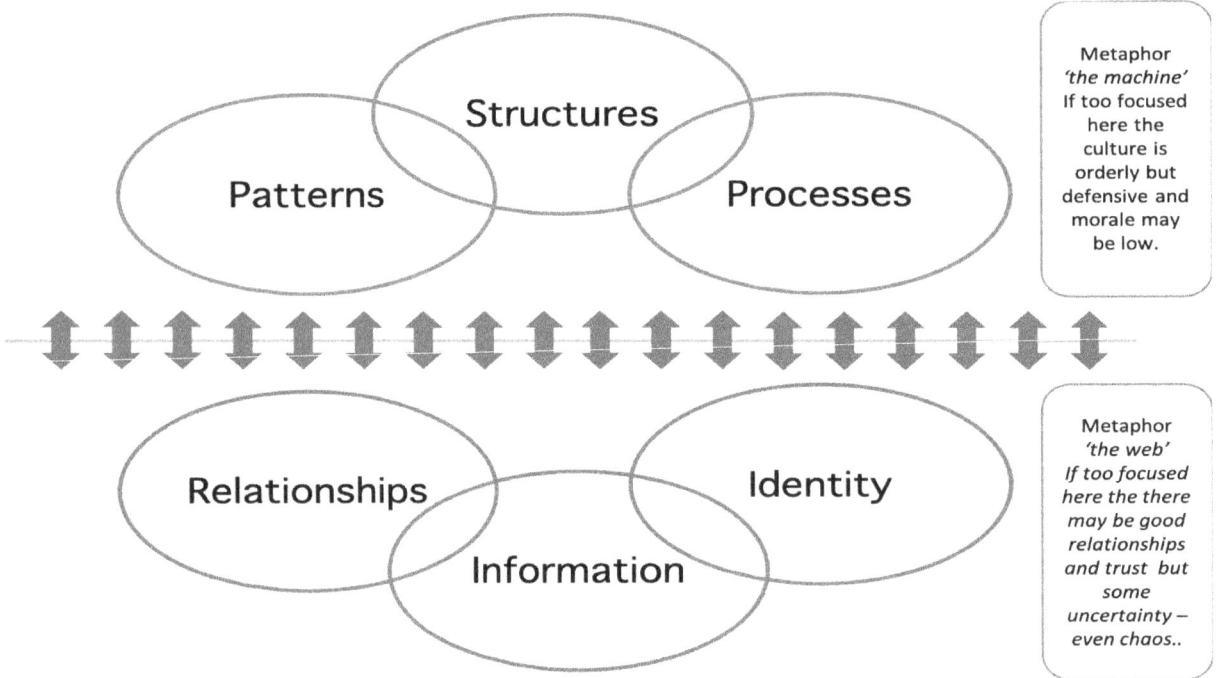

Structures

Patterns

Processes

Metaphor *'the machine'* If too focused here the culture is orderly but defensive and morale may be low.

Relationships

Identity

Information

Metaphor *'the web'* If too focused here the there may be good relationships and trust but some uncertainty – even chaos..

Detail of the Above and Below the Green Line model:

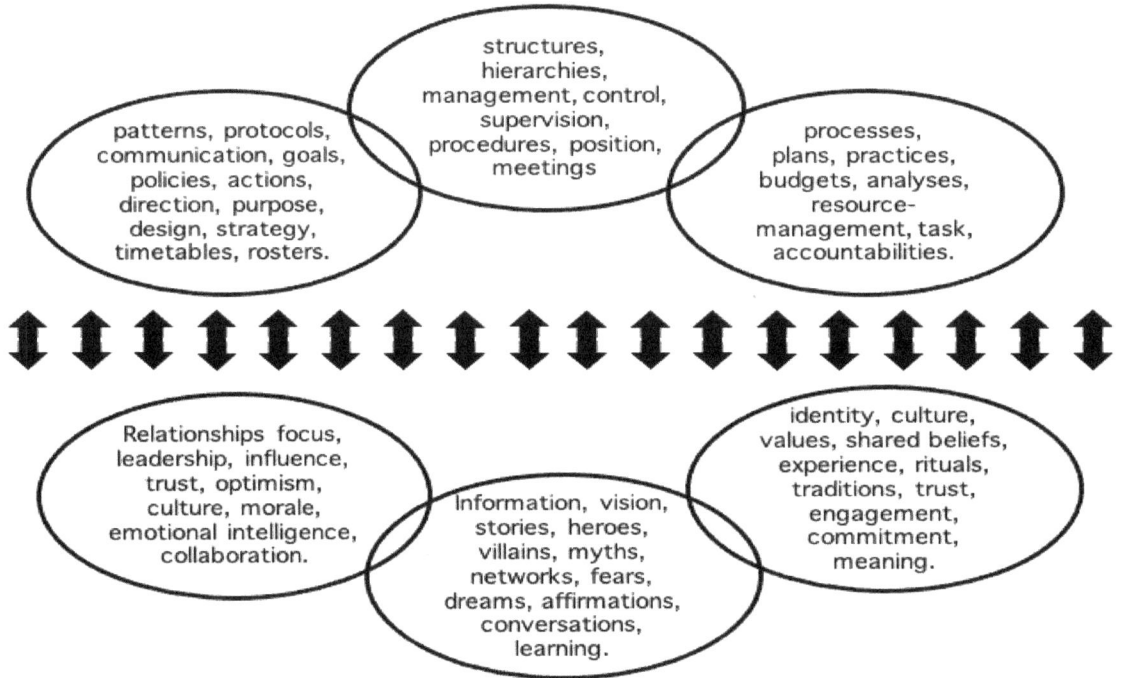

structures, hierarchies, management, control, supervision, procedures, position, meetings

patterns, protocols, communication, goals, policies, actions, direction, purpose, design, strategy, timetables, rosters.

processes, plans, practices, budgets, analyses, resource-management, task, accountabilities.

Relationships focus, leadership, influence, trust, optimism, culture, morale, emotional intelligence, collaboration.

Information, vision, stories, heroes, villains, myths, networks, fears, dreams, affirmations, conversations, learning.

identity, culture, values, shared beliefs, experience, rituals, traditions, trust, engagement, commitment, meaning.

The 'Product' of our school

Purpose: This is another way of helping the team to think about their role and purpose in the school.

Process:

1. The activity commences with the presentation of a provocative proposition: 'Like every industry, Education has a product. As educators we can't become more productive until we are very certain about what our product is'.
2. Team members work in pairs to discuss what the product of the school is: they are challenged to create a statement about the product that is specific and measurable.
3. After a few minutes each pair joins another pair to write an agreed product statement.
4. The groups exchange or circulate their product statements. Each group adds comments such as 'like', disagree', 'this would be a better way to put this' to the statements of other groups. The purpose of the comments is to help the originating group refine and sharpen their statement.
5. When each group gets their own statement back they read all the comments and use these to improve their product statement.
6. All of the statements are compared. Common or attractive aspects of school productivity are extracted and adopted by the whole group.
7. The product statement is displayed.

Reflective Questions:

- Was this a useful way for us to think about our purpose?
- When we describe our work in terms of productivity, who are the most productive members of the school community? – Leaders? Teachers? Parents?
- Has this changed the way we see our role as team members or leaders.

Section Five

Team Deliberation and Decision-Making

The way in which a team discusses and deliberates on issues and options defines the culture of the team. A functional team has a preference for open and searching processes to underpin their leadership and decision-making. Many examples of such processes are included in this section.

The way the team makes decisions is also critical to its performance. It's unrealistic to divorce the way that a team makes decisions from the way that the team functions. Teams that have been formed to be powerful coalitions of thought and action will encourage energetic individual contribution and personal engagement. Members of such a team will expect a significant voice in team decisions.

This section begins with a review of decision-making processes and a clear advocacy for those that are closest to consensus. Decisions made together engender the commitment that is so important to team success.

In this section several processes for reaching consensus are described, as well as a range of other decision-making, problem-solving and substantive conversation tools which are so thorough that consensus often emerges from them - twenty-four activities in all!

The last chapter is a series of Perceptual Positions activities. Gregory Bateson[1] famously observed that: "Wisdom comes from multiple perspectives." Learning to deliberately use each of the four Perceptual Positions enriches team interaction and enhances team decisions. When the members of a team can turn their attention away from their own thoughts and preferences (which is 1st position) and attend to the other three positions, they are embracing the wisdom to which Bateson refers.

[1] *Gregory Bateson was a charismatic and insightful polymath whose writing and ideas spanned many disciplines. His most famous book was 'Steps to an Ecology of Mind'.*

Decision-making
The Road to Consensus

Purpose: To examine the **decision-making options** available to teams and review the 'pros and cons' of each.

Processes: Conduct a reflective review of team decision making practices using the passage below:

Let's look at the choices facing for example, a school Principal working with her or his executive team. The Principal has four possible ways of working with the team:

1. The team can be **informed**. The Principal or Senior Executive members decide on a course of action and communicate their decision to the remaining executive who are expected to support the decision. Discussion is usually limited to the ways that the team members can implement the decisions that have been made. If this is the team's usual way of doing business then team members will rarely exhibit high levels of commitment or feel personally accountable for outcomes.

2. The first of the truly participative options is **Consultation.** The opinions and ideas of the team are canvassed and the Principal makes the decision after hearing the contribution of team-members.. With this option there is rarely deep discussion or lively debate. Sometimes this option for making the decision is an unavoidable last resort: e.g. when there is significant unresolvable disagreement among team members and a decision cannot be deferred. This practice is ultimately unsatisfactory for team members and for the culture of team, because the decision is still not made by the team. The commitment of group members is likely to be uncertain if this way of deciding is used often.

3. **Participation** is a better option. It implies that team members are involved, not only in the discussion and discourse related to a decision, but also in choosing the way that the situation is resolved. However, the final decision may still be left to conventional voting or to a decision by the team leader. Although this way of making a decision will not necessarily engage the commitment of the whole team, it can work well enough when there are high levels of trust between team members and Principal, and when there is too little time to reach consensus

4. The most engaging way to make teams decisions is through full **Collaboration**, aiming to achieve a consensus decision. The whole team is responsible for engaging in the discussion, debating the issues, deciding on how to resolve differences and in finding a

mutually agreeable resolution. This option often takes longest and requires some skill to achieve BUT, because the aim of consensus is some version of 'we all agree', it is the decision-making process that is most likely to engage the commitment of the whole team. When consensus is achieved team members are almost certain to be fully committed, will hold themselves accountable for the consequences of the decision, and will devote themselves to achieving the desired results..

However, although reaching **consensus** is often discussed as if it was as simple as finding an option which every team member agrees with – it rarely is! More usually the process used will result in a choice that is: '*best we can do*' or '*what we can all agree to commit to and take action upon*'.

The diagram on the next page illustrates some of the processes and strategies that may be employed to achieve consensus. Any of these processes is an improvement on simple 'Yes' or' No' voting. Though binary voting is the most common and fastest way of resolving an issue it can result in 51% in favour and 49% against – far from the best option for team cohesion or individual commitment!

Reflective Questions:
- What will we have to be prepared to invest in the deliberations of this team if we want to make collaborative decisions?
- What might we have to give up as strong individuals in order to achieve genuine collaboration?
- Is here a downside to making decisions with which we all agree?
- When we come to agreement in our meetings how will we respond when the decision is criticised by staff members?

Consensus Decision Making

Desirable: because it generates greatest commitment
...... Not always possible

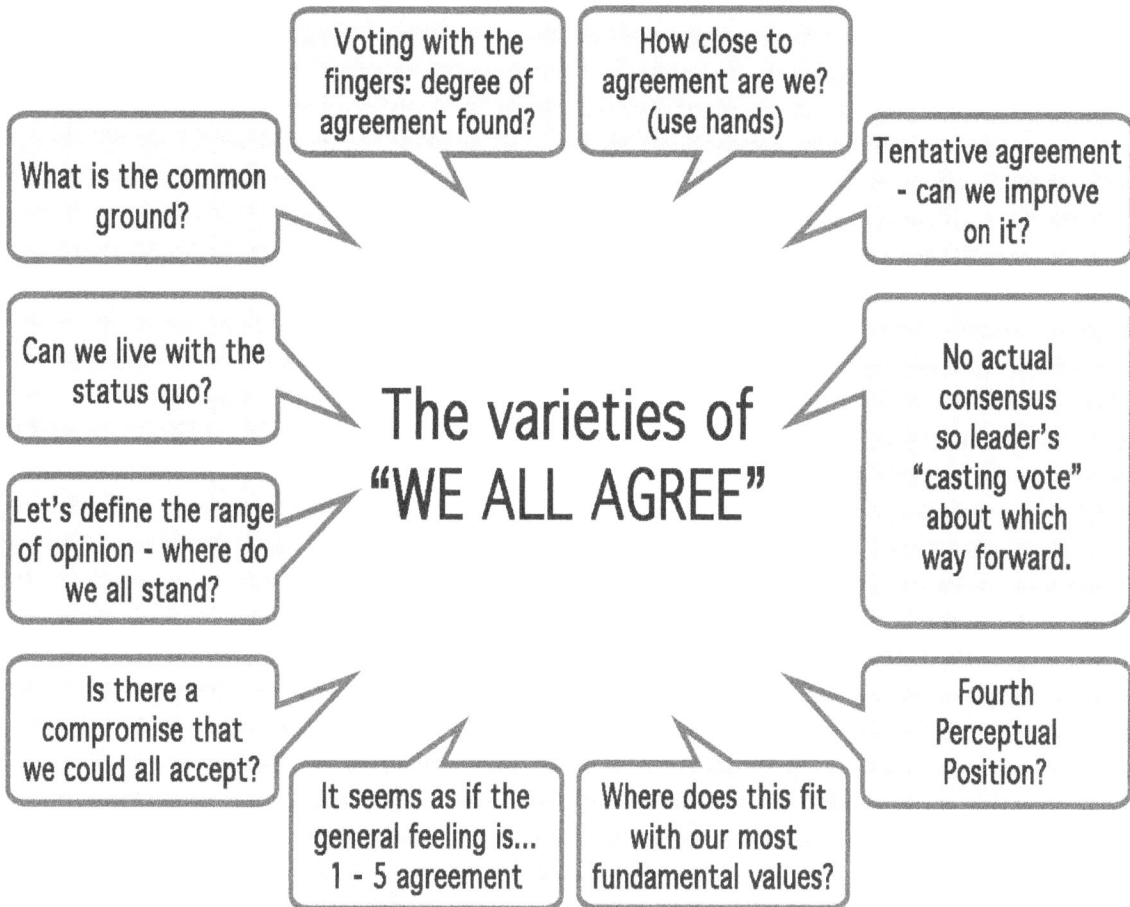

Voting with the fingers: degree of agreement found?

How close to agreement are we? (use hands)

What is the common ground?

Tentative agreement - can we improve on it?

Can we live with the status quo?

The varieties of "WE ALL AGREE"

No actual consensus so leader's "casting vote" about which way forward.

Let's define the range of opinion - where do we all stand?

Is there a compromise that we could all accept?

Fourth Perceptual Position?

It seems as if the general feeling is... 1 - 5 agreement

Where does this fit with our most fundamental values?

When no consensus is reached:
Do we need to make a decision now?
Is there some information that we could gather to help us move closer to agreement?

5-finger Voting: A consensus-seeking model.

(As introduced to me by Joy Verrinder.)

Purpose: This activity supports the use of consensus decision making. At any point in a discussion about the best way forward, the degree of agreement of the team can be tested and made visible.

Process: As illustrated below.

The team should thoroughly discuss the process before using it to ensure that everyone understands the significance of each of the 6 levels of 'willingness to agree'.

5 fingers		Fully in favour of this proposal. Convinced this is best way to proceed. I am committed
4 fingers		In favour of the proposal. Ready to commit.
3 fingers		Not completely convinced but I will trust the group and commit to following through with the team's decision.
2 fingers		Not convinced that we can't improve on this – but not opposed. Would be happier if we could talk more. I will support the team's decision.
1 finger		I am presently opposed to this and will need persuasion to move from here – however if I am alone in my scepticism I will bow to the wisdom of the group.
Fist		We're on the wrong track here. I wish to offer or re-submit an alternative we should consider. (If anyone votes "fist", the alternative is always heard and considered before returning to the original proposal)

5-finger voting can be used at various stages of a team discussion. Sometimes when an issue is first canvassed and a proposal is made, a quick 5-finger vote can determine the spread of opinion on the team. This is useful because it will determine the way in which the proposal is considered. For example:

- If almost everyone votes 3 or lower then there is very little enthusiasm for the proposal on the table and it will need to be refined, better explained or dropped.
- If there is strong support – mostly 4's and 5's but with a few 1's or fists then the focus will be on the objections of the outliers so that the team can address their issues of concern.

Even though this form of 'voting' is far superior to the 'YES – NO' version it will rarely result in everyone voting 4 and 5. This is where the 'Is this the best we can do for now' question will be put to the team.

Reflective Questions: Usually only necessary early in the team's use of this practice.
- 'What will it mean if we all vote 2?'
- 'What will we do if there is polarization?' (4&5 v 1&2)
- What information does this process give us that we would not get from simpler processes such as conventional voting?
- How can we use this process to focus our discussions as well as to come to agreement?

Does this FIT our W.O.C.?

Purpose: To simplify team decisions by checking to see which options are aligned with the 'Window of Certainty'© which has previously been created. As the Window of Certainty was a collaborative construction by the team (or the whole staff) many consensus decisions emerge easily by referring to the 'Window' and preferring the decision or direction that is the 'best fit' for the W.O.C.

Equipment: A copy of the 'Window of Certainty'© for the school or team.

Process:
1. The Proposal or alternative proposals are clearly presented to the team.
2. Team members ask whatever questions are needed for the proposal or proposals to be absolutely clear.
3. The Team now works together to answer these 4 questions about the proposal (or proposals):
     I.   Will this advance our achievement of the school's vision and purpose?
     II.   Will taking the action proposed lead to the achievement of one or more of the outcomes we are working towards?
     III. Do the proposed strategies accord with our stated beliefs?
     IV.   Do the behaviours associated with the proposal align with the values-in-action that we chose to underpin our culture.
4. If the proposal (or one of the proposals) is a good fit for the 'Window of Certainty'© there will always be further questions (such as: 'will we have to stop doing something else to take this on?' or 'will the timing of this initiative be appropriate in the present context?') However, using the four "Window of Certainty' questions usually clarifies the major issues involved.

Reflective Questions: - Are we working within the boundaries we have created?
  -   Is there sufficient autonomy within the boundaries to encourage initiative?

Reality Thinking!

(A process for team decision making based on Dr. William Glasser's *Reality Therapy*.)

Purpose: To clarify the goal or outcome that the team wants to achieve and to generate realistic options for effective action.

Equipment: Knowledge of the model and the team-leader's well-developed questioning skills and ability to paraphrase team member contributions.

Process: This practice uses the procedures for change as illustrated:

1. The team leader uses the process to assist the team to clearly identify a goal or outcome, evaluate past efforts and explore new options.
2. If there is no positive goal, use the 'flipping' strategy (next page) to make sure that the team is pursuing a positive want.
3. Ask the Doing and Evaluation questions several times to ensure that the team has identified and evaluated everything they previously attempted in pursuing this goal.

An open and supportive team culture
(vulnerability-based trust)

W • What do we want? What's our goal?

D • What have we been doing to get what we want?

E • Has it been working? Has anything worked?

O • What other options (choices) do we have?

P • What actions will we take? (S.M.A.R.T)

4. When all options are considered and an action is decided on, ensure that it is: Specific; Measurable; Attractive; Realistic and Time-framed.

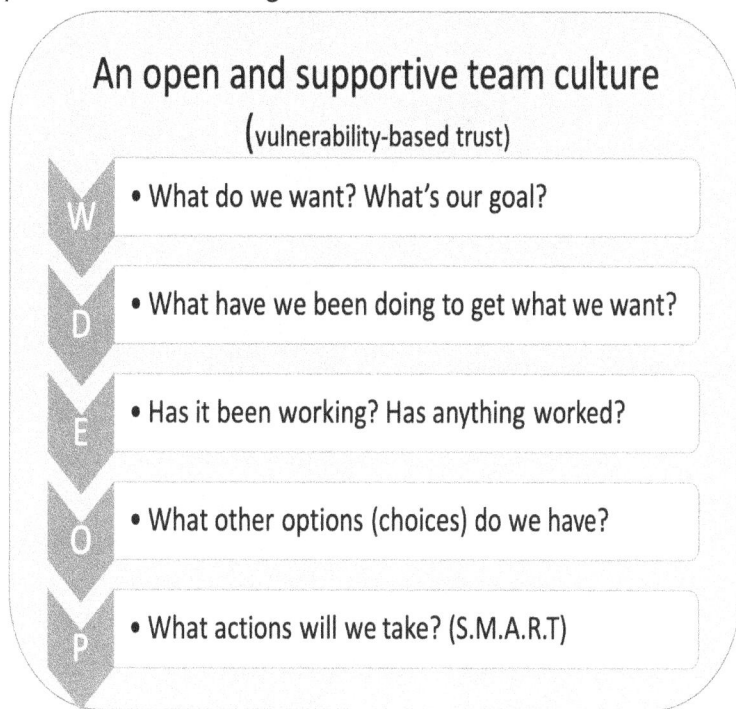

Reflective Questions: Did we stick to the process?

FLIPPING (positive re-framing)

(as taught by Judy Hatswell of Judy Hatswell and Associates)

Purpose: To ensure that team discussions are solution-focused rather than problem oriented. Team members often become very focused on a problem they perceive – which is something that that they don't want. However, a useful solution rarely arises from focusing on the problem. Use 'Flipping' to focus team conversations on the solution – the positive want or goal.

Process: The process of flipping involves taking the negative value of a question or statement and flipping it to the positive. The process is based on our knowledge that a 'don't want' always presupposes a 'want'.

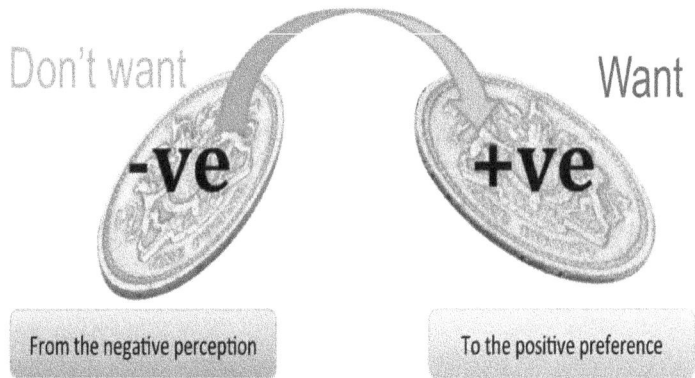

Don't want

-ve

From the negative perception

Want

+ve

To the positive preference

1. **Acknowledge the team's concern.** There will be an emotion in the negative perception. Use empathic listening to recognise and acknowledge the emotion and the concern (the 'FLIP' is easiest when you have heard and understood the value behind the concern).
2. Look for the value in the negative statement and use it in the flip. The main challenge of the flip is that language is often ambiguous so you may have to 'guess' at the underlying value. However, it does not matter if you get it wrong – you will be heard as attributing a positive value to the other person.
3. The intention of the flip is to turn a negative perception or problem statement into a positive goal or preferred situation.
4. Resist the temptation to use the flip as a contradiction to a team member's statement. Appearing to contradict creates resistance.
5. The table on the next page illustrates some common 'Flips' or positive reframes.
6. If you are not sure how to positively reframe a negative perception or proposition ask the team "If this was not a concern and if everything was as we would like it to be, what would be happening?" The team will offer a suitable reframe (flip) for you.

Negative perception (frustration)	Positive value (the want or goal)
Someone or some group is: Isolated, left out, clashing, disconnected, unwanted, ignored, disengaged, at-odds.	**What we want is to:** Connect or engage them, involve or include them, care, resolve issues, restore harmony.
Someone or some group is: Helpless, incompetent, not respected, fragile, frustrated, unsuccessful, unskilled unsure, uncertain, unappreciated.	**We want them to be (to feel)** Confident, composed, capable, respected, valued, competent, powerful, successful, important, thriving, effective, skilled.
Someone or some group is: Constrained, limited, coerced, forced, obstructed, restricted, reliant, dependent.	**We want them to be :** Autonomous, self-determined, free, willing, independent, self-sufficient, in control.
Someone or some group is: Bored, uninterested, uninvolved, finding dull or tedious, indifferent, disengaged.	**We want them to be:** Learning, enjoying, stimulated, interested, entertained, challenged, having fun, engaged.
Someone or some group is: Fearful, threatened, bullied, insecure, coerced, frightened, apprehensive, cowed.	**We want them to be:** Safe, confident, protected, trusting, brave, calm, optimistic, hopeful, self-assured.

7. Once you have a positive goal, use any of the processes for open discussion and consensus decision-making.

- **Reflective Questions:** Did we focus on what we want rather than what we want to avoid?
- Was focusing on a solution rather than the problem conducive to resolving the issue or addressing the problem?

Catering for Type Preferences

Purpose: To make the team aware of the different type preferences that are likely to affect the openness and effectiveness of team deliberation.

The interactions and communication of team members will benefit from allowing for the differences in personality as revealed by the four dichotomies.

Processes:
1. Initiate discussions to help team members understand the preferences associated with each of these dichotomies:

Extraverted Types
Group size irrelevant.
Need opportunities to think out loud. Sharing and discussion in groups provides opportunity to refine their thinking.

Introverted types
Individual quiet time to think is appreciated. Small group processing is important. Like to know in advance what will be discussed and why.

Sensing Types
Like to work from concrete information and make sense of issues through data, facts, evidence.

Intuitive Types
Like to see the connections between issues and events and get the 'big picture' reasons for actions.

Thinking Types
Like critical analysis. Make decisions based on logic, rules or precedent and focus on fairness and equity.

Feeling Types
Consideration for others is important. Like to make decisions based on how people will be affected.

Judging Types
Like to be organised. make decisions early and plan well ahead. Dislike uncertainty and last-minute change.

Perceiving types
Like to make sure that all information and many options are considered. Usually flexible and adaptable.

Even if the team has no prior knowledge of personality preferences (and have not used the MBTI profile instrument) the differences described above will usually help them identify and nominate their own preferences.

For more information about the MBTI go to: *www.futureshape.com.au* or to the website of the Myers-Briggs Company.

2. Organise team meetings in ways that will cater for each of the dichotomies without having to treat different preference groups differently (as below).
3. The team meeting processes that are most likely to be inclusive for all personality types are as follows:
   o Publish the agenda in advance;
   o Sit in a circle so that everyone can make eye contact with all team members and so that the team can easily break up into smaller groups;
   o Use small groups of 3-5 for discussion and processing of information (suits both extraverted and introverted preference types);
   o Provide as much evidence as possible to support team deliberation and decision making;
   o Ensure that the 'Why' of all decisions is available in both detail and big picture;
   o If possible, leave time between the discussion of an issue and any decision made;
   o When a significant change is proposed allow plenty of lead time for deliberation and discussion;
   o Provide processes and opportunities for team members to communicate with everyone who will be affected by decisions;
   o Institute processes that allow the team to receive feedback on any proposals from those that they represent.

Reflective Questions:

- Did everyone feel that they had an opportunity to participate fully in our deliberations?
- Was the meeting conducted in an inclusive way that invited all team members to have their say?
- Is there any way that we can improve the inclusivity of our meeting processes?

The PARETO Provocation

Purpose: To use the 'Pareto Principle' as a reflective or analytic tool that can guide the team in its allocation of time, energy and resources.

Process:
1. The team works as individuals in the first phase and is asked to consider each of the Pareto-related questions in turn:
    - *Which 20% of the practices in our school are producing 80% of our successful outcomes?*
    - *Where in our school are we devoting a large % of time, energy and resources to produce a very low % of our success?*
2. After 10 to 12 minutes of individual consideration team members pair off and share their thoughts and decide what to contribute to the whole team discussion.
    In the whole team, use this (or any other) process for sharing the input from groups:

    (How ➜ What ➜ Why ➜ What ➜ How)
- **How** is the 20% of effective time producing so much of our success? OR **How** are we devoting a dis-proportionate level % of unproductive time?
- **What** are we doing that is working so well in this productive 20%? OR **What** are we doing that takes so much time but is unproductive?
- **Why** are we only allocating 20% of time to productive activity? OR **Why** are we allocating so much time to unproductive activity?
- **What** could we do differently in either case?
- **How** will we put our changed priorities into action?

Reflective Questions:
- In what way was this activity challenging for us?
- Was the result of using this process surprising to you?
- Is there a way that we can use this kind of reflective process to usefully challenge our habitual priorities?

Note: The Pareto Principle, named after economist Vilfredo Pareto, states that 80% of consequences come from 20% of causes.

The Learning Cycle

Based on *'Matthew Miles Learning Cycle'*. (as described to me by Ken Gilbert).

Equipment: a 'Matthew Miles' Learning Cycle' page for each team member.

Purpose: When the best course of action is not clear, the cycle offers a process for initiating and reviewing experimental solutions.

Process: Follow the cycle below

The Learning Cycle: From Matthew Miles: "Learning to Work in Groups"
Always finish the Cycle!

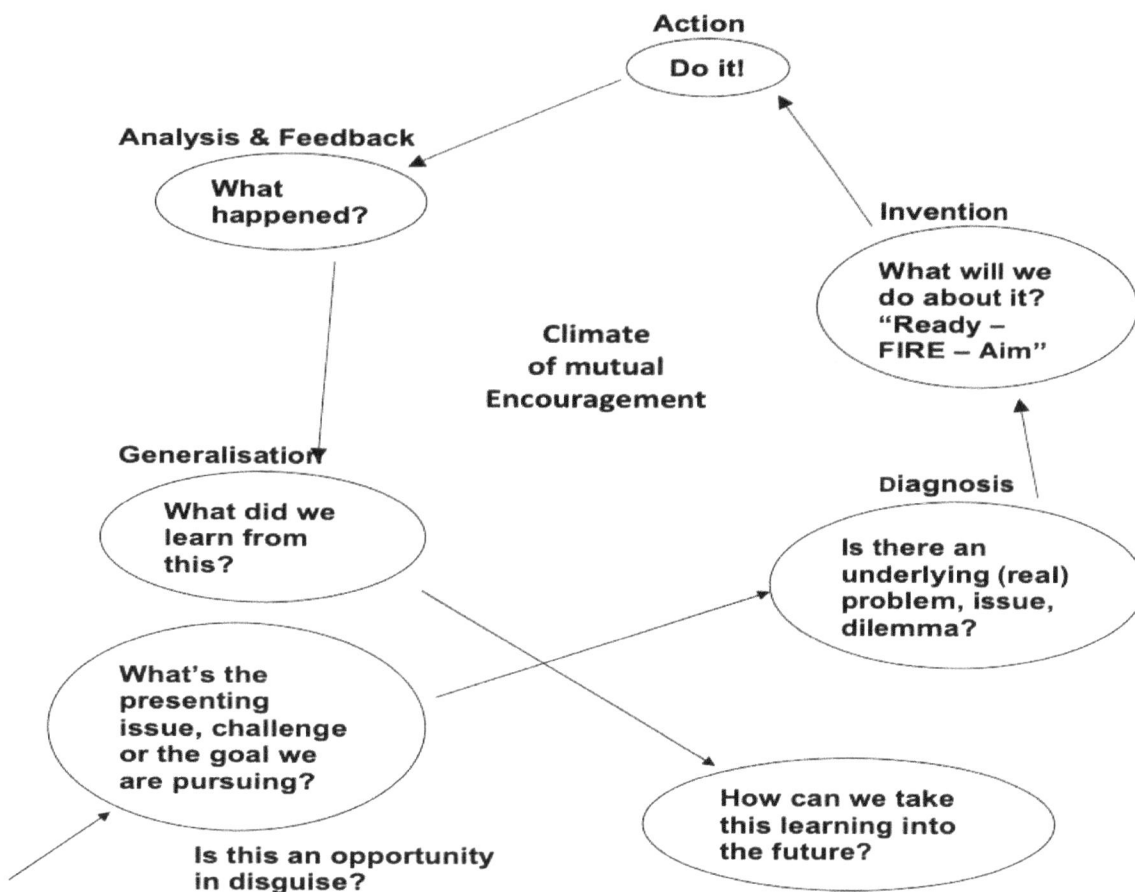

Action
Do it!

Analysis & Feedback
What happened?

Invention
What will we do about it? "Ready – FIRE – Aim"

Climate of mutual Encouragement

Generalisation
What did we learn from this?

Diagnosis
Is there an underlying (real) problem, issue, dilemma?

What's the presenting issue, challenge or the goal we are pursuing?

How can we take this learning into the future?

Is this an opportunity in disguise?

Reflective Questions: are embedded in the cycle.

The Rational Change Process

Purpose: To make sure that any change that the team implements is **rational** – i.e. that it takes the team from a situation that is unsatisfactory (at least in part) to one that is closer to ideal.

Equipment: You can use the template on the next page.

Process:

1. Perceptions

What are we presently doing?
What is not working?
What would we like to keep?

THE GAP

2. Wants

What do we want – a realistic picture of how things will be better if we change. – include positive aspects of the present.

List all of the DIFFERENCES between what we are doing and our preferred future:

- -
- -
- -

Apply knowledge (research) and experience to each difference. What change will work.

Create mental models that provide reasons for replacement actions and strategies.

What are:
The quick wins?
The longer-term changes needed?
The key paradigms, processes and practices to change?
The mental models underpinning the differences?
The new capabilities needed?
Our strategic change plans?

A model for Rational Change Developed by Rob Stones from Dr Glasser's Reality Therapy

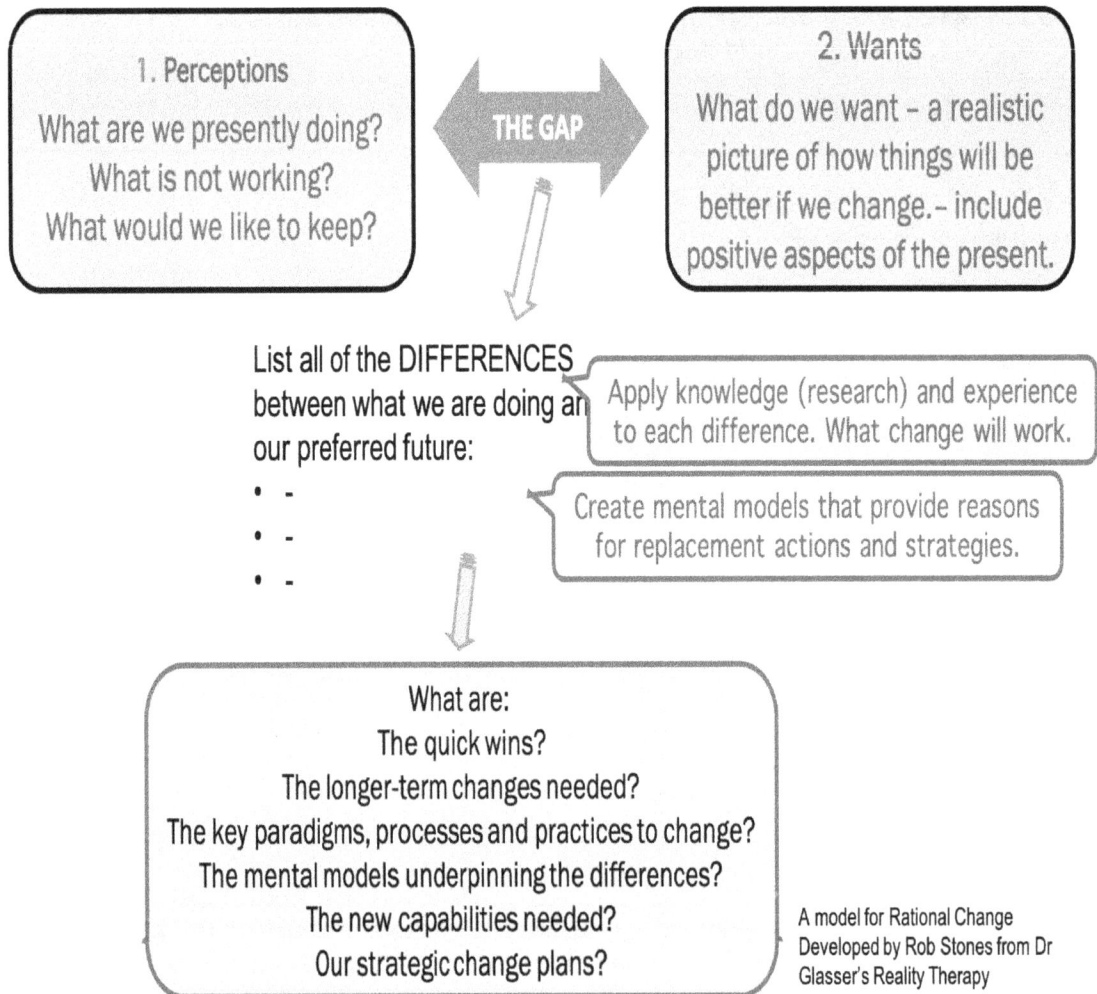

Reflective Questions to ask include:
- Have we retained all of the productivity that existed before the change?
- Do transparent mental models exist to justify the change?
- Are we certain that the improvement will justify the effort needed?

A Template for the 'Rational Change Model':

1. Present perception of the situation:
Describe, in detail, the present situation - which you would like to change.

2. What we want:
Describe in detail the realistic Ideal situation.

The GAP

3. Differences
List all of the differences between 1 and 2

4 Actions
Choose actions that will have the most leverage for getting to what you want + some 'quick wins' to demonstrate progress and generate confidence.

A Meeting Agenda

Purpose: To focus the agenda of team meetings on the purpose and function of the School. This is important because meeting agendas derived from the usual business model are not always a good fit for schools. The meeting agenda process described below helps to keep the team focused on what happens *between* team meetings – not what happens in the meeting. The effectiveness of the team is always determined by what team members do between meetings.

Equipment: A prepared agenda based on the Agenda script provided.

Process: This team meeting agenda is based on a process that helps the team remain focused on the actions they take, or learning they need, between team meetings.

Agenda:

1. **Starter or connection activity:** A transition between the busy-ness of the day and more reflective team mode.
2. **Follow-Up:** What commitments were made at the last meeting and what actions have been taken as a result? This item should include succinct reports from every team member who accepted accountability for taking action that is due to have been completed. (This is not a 'report from everyone' session – it is a deliberate follow-up to commitments made!).
3. **Progress:** What progress has been made on each of the student focused outcome areas of our school plan and explicit improvement agenda. This item keeps the school plan (created around the schools 'Window of Certainty' and key accountabilities) front and centre in every meeting.
4. **Where are we stuck?** Identify areas where there is no progress or where progress is slow. Do we need to re-strategise? (see the Manning Model page 119).
   Is there anything we or our staff need to learn in order to make progress?
5. **Learning:** What have we learned (or discovered that we need to learn) since our last meeting, that is needed if we are to accomplish our purpose as a team? (Base this on the successive key questions that can be derived from Helen Timperley's improvement cycle):
   - What knowledge and skills do our students need to be successful?
   - What knowledge and skills do teachers need to optimise student success?
   - What knowledge and skills do we need to support teachers and their learning?
6. **What's working?** What have we been doing that is working well to achieve our purpose? How can we support and extend this success? (And conversely, is there

anything that we are doing that is not helping to optimise student learning or which may be discouraging students from achieving their personal best?)

7. **Minimise Distractions:** Are we allocating time and energy to anything that is distracting us from our core purpose? What do we notice? Can we minimise distractions for our teachers and students? - or for ourselves? (Note that there are always distractions. It's not always possible for the team to avoid these but it is important to minimise the leakage of energy, time and morale that these create!)

8. **Anything else?** Should be left until last and kept to a minimum.

9. **Conclusion - Summarise Decisions and Commitments:**
   - What decisions have we made today that will help optimise student success in our school?
   - What commitments have individuals, or the team made in this meeting that will be followed up next time we meet (these will include the commitment to communicate the decisions and expectations of the team).

Debriefing Questions: Important questions to ask after meetings:
- Were we focused on key purpose today?
- Are we holding each other accountable for pursuing the school's explicit purpose and improvement agenda?
- How well did we manage ourselves and display commitment to our team norms today?

Note: You will not necessarily have items in every agenda item in every meeting. However, items 2 & 3 should always be included.

RPD: Recognition-Primed decision-making

Based on Sources of Power: How People Make Decisions - Gary Klein.

Purpose: To use a process for coming to a decision that is skeptical of formal decision-making practices. The essence of RPD in education is to draw on the experience of leaders / teachers, and their knowledge of how people will respond, rather than a laborious exploration of options. RPD aims to avoid the 'paralysis of analysis' by helping team members recognise and act in accordance with previous successful experience.

Process:

1. The context and the purpose for making a decision are briefly discussed so that everyone understands why this decision is important now.
2. The focus is on actions taken. Team members use imagination and intuition rather than 'logic' to visualise how potential actions will be carried out.
3. They test these mental simulations against possible consequences using - '**if** we do this **then** what?' based on their expertise and previous experience. It's not just the immediate consequence they are visualizing but the consequences that flow from those immediate consequence.
4. They also ask themselves questions such as:
   - Is this like something we have found a solution to before?
   - How is this like previous actions we have taken successfully?
   - Which actions involve the least complexity and unpredictability?
5. The consensus process for agreeing a decision will be either:
   - What does experience tell us about which action will succeed?
   - Is this the best we can do right now?

Debriefing Questions: Because the immediate process is action-oriented rather than reflective the de-briefing should occur as an after-action-analysis:

- What did we learn that will serve us well in the future?
- What would we adjust if we face these circumstances again?
- If we had taken other actions what would have been different?

The 1% Exploration

Purpose: To encourage the habit of continuous improvement. Based on the initiative pioneered by the Toyota Motor Company, this practice encourages every team member (every staff member) to suggest small improvements to any process, practice, procedure or system that is operating in the school.

Instead of thinking 'someone should do something about this', everyone who believes that they can see a way of improving the way the school is going about things, even in a very small way, is asked to fill in a 1% card and submit it to the school executive. Notice that this practice works in a significantly different way to a 'suggestion box' which is often used to identify problems. All 1% improvement ideas are solutions!

Process:

1. '1% improvement' cards are available throughout the school. They have only simple headings:
   - Identify what can be improved _____;
   - What is the 1% improvement you are suggesting _____;
   - How will it work _____;
   - Please provide your name so that the executive can ask for further information and work with you to put your solution into practice.

2. All 1% suggestions are considered by the executive leader responsible for the procedure that can be improved (or by the executive team). The secret of the success of the program is for **every 1% improvement to be implemented if it can be!**

3. The person who suggested the 1% improvement will work in partnership with an executive leader to implement the initiative and to take responsibility for evaluating the success of the initiative.

Debriefing /follow up:
- Keep records of all 1% initiatives and the affect they have.
- Report regularly to the staff on the number of and success of 1% initiatives.

9 Mind Tools for team discussion

Purpose: to provide the team with a repertoire of processes for discussion, analysis, sharing opinions or team reflection. Most of these can be conducted as both whole-group and small group processes. Using processes such as these will encourage deeper thinking, creative ideas, greater openness and initiative.

Think-Pair-Share:

This a simple but effective way to open up cognition and involve everyone in the team in making a contribution. As the name implies, the process is simple:
1. Individuals consider a proposal or an issue for themselves;
2. After a short time, they discuss their ideas with a team-mate;
3. All pairs contribute to the whole team discussion.

Define-Personalise-Challenge:

A process that helps the team to work through a proposal or situation by asking team members to:
1. Define the problem or explain the situation with as much clarity as possible;
2. Say what the issue means to them. Ask "How are you personally affected?"
3. Challenge each person to suggest an opportunity or initiative that could come from the situation.

Connect-Extend-Challenge:

This is another way of examining an issue or opportunity:
1. How is this connected to something we are familiar with or an issue we have dealt with before?
2. If we were to extend our thinking to the very best of very worst that might result from the issue facing us, what would those polarities be?
3. What is the biggest challenge for us in this situation? How can we confront it head on?

The 5 Why's:

A strategy that is a simple process for digging deeply into any proposal.

When a proposal or suggestion is offered to the team, members of the team clarify the proposal by asking 'Why'. Whatever the answer is, the team's response is to ask another 'Why' and so on. By the time the 5th 'Why' is reached the rationale for the proposal should be very clear.

The Reflective Review:
Can be used to review any situation that the team wants to learn from, whether the outcome was positive or not.
1. Reflect – team members ask themselves or each other 'what happened'?
2. Interpret – Each person or group contributes a response to the question 'What did it mean' or 'How were we affected?'
3. Apply – How can we apply what we have learned from what happened?
4. Engage – take action on the possible application.

Ready-Fire-Aim:
When the team is not sure about exactly what to do and team members are unable to predict the consequences of proposals this strategy is both an antidote to 'paralysis by analysis' and a sound way of building in after-action-reflection. The steps are:
1. **Ready:** prepare by examining the situation and choosing the course of action that seems most likely to succeed given the limited information available;
2. **Fire: Do it** – implement the action!
3. **Aim:** Now use the information from the action to re-focus and refine. What happened, what worked, what did not work, how can we improve the actions; what do we now know that will help us do even better. Now fire again!

Steps to a solution:
A process that takes the team through 6 steps from the statement of a problem to a solution:
1. What's the problem? – state the problem clearly;
2. Why is it a problem?
3. What does a solution look like?
4. What else is possible?
5. What may be the unintended consequences?
6. When will we act?

When action has been taken and the solution is implemented it is reviewed: What did we learn? What will we do differently next time?

Reverse Brainstorm:
Most teams are familiar with brainstorming (uncritical suggestions that are collected and reviewed in a search for a creative solution).

Reverse brainstorming also tends to lead to very creative and unexpected solutions by asking team members to consider how what they are doing might have its own failure built into it!

Brainstorming questions I have used include:

- If we were to implement this policy in a way that makes no difference at all how will we do it?
- If our aim was to make sure that students are bored with learning, what pedagogical practices would we employ?
- If we wanted to make sure our students developed no self-discipline or personal responsibility what would we do?
- If we wanted to make our stage meetings as boring and irrelevant as possible, how would we do it?

It's amazing the insights that come thick and fast when you conduct a reverse brainstorm!!

The Pre-Mortem:
A pre-action reflection that is a very simple but often powerful way of anticipating (and guarding against) the negative consequences of a change or new action. Use it whenever you are about to commit significant energy, resources and time to something new and different.

1. Ask the team the pre-mortem question:

   "if we were sitting here in a few months, time looking back at everything that had gone wrong in our implementation of this change, what would we be saying to each other?

2. The intuition of the team members, and the unspoken doubts that team members had, but did not previously mention, should now all be accepted and considered.
3. The team can now consider how to anticipate and avoid the predicted consequences by modifying the intended strategies.

Strategic Thinking
(Derived from Tony Manning's 7P Model).

Purpose: - To help the team to plan with a focus on the elements of strategy.
- Use when a planned strategy is not achieving the intended outcome.

Equipment: Copies of the model

Process – Use my Adaptation of the Manning Strategic Model as illustrated below:

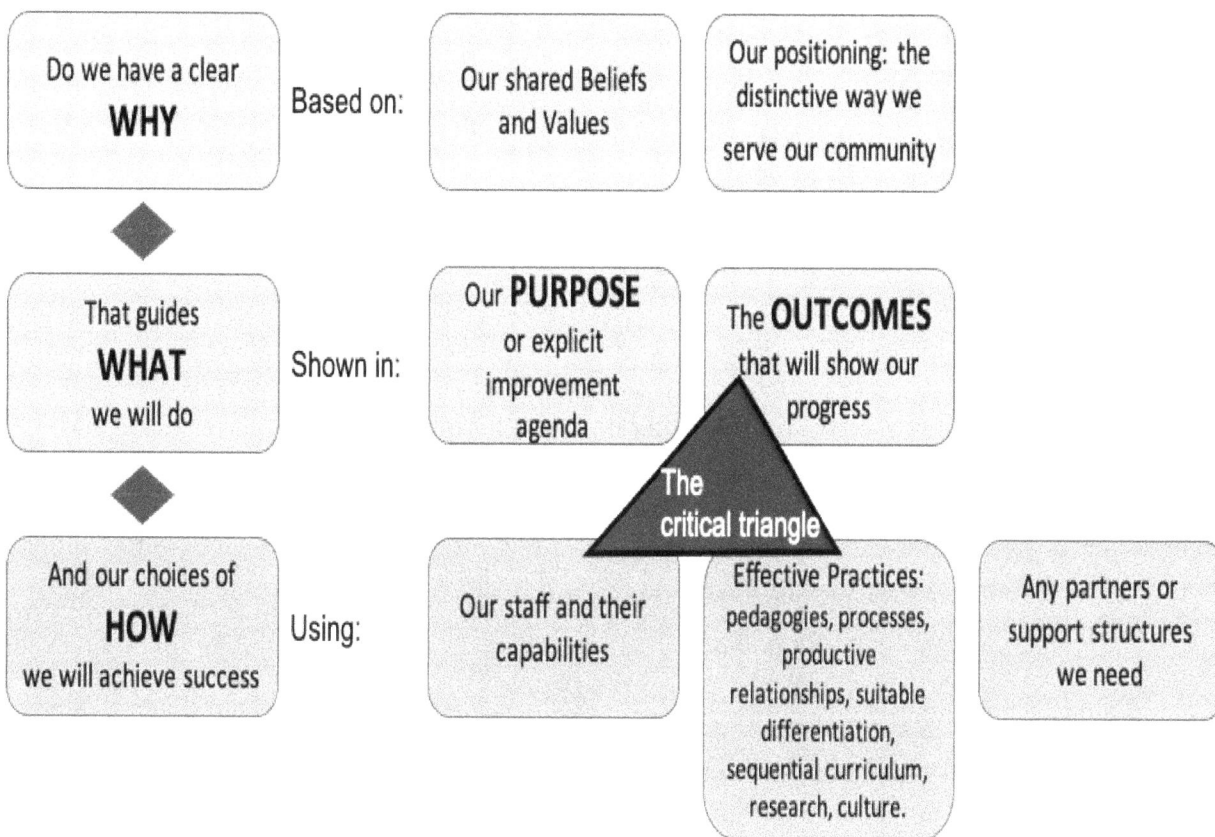

Do we have a clear **WHY**	Based on:	Our shared Beliefs and Values	Our positioning: the distinctive way we serve our community

That guides **WHAT** we will do	Shown in:	Our **PURPOSE** or explicit improvement agenda	The **OUTCOMES** that will show our progress

The critical triangle

And our choices of **HOW** we will achieve success	Using:	Our staff and their capabilities	Effective Practices: pedagogies, processes, productive relationships, suitable differentiation, sequential curriculum, research, culture.	Any partners or support structures we need

1. Ensure that strategic direction is based on a solid 'Why' and that the Purpose and Outcomes are clearly stated (What).
2. Work in the Critical Triangle (Capabilities – Practices – Outcomes). If there is no progress towards the outcomes, then ask yourself either:
   - What practices or actions do we need to vary?
   - What capability must we develop in ourselves and or our teachers?
3. Take action.

De-briefing questions are built into the model.

Distilling - write and pass on.

Purpose: To extend or refine the team's collective thinking in a way that is sometimes more productive that discussion or a brainstorm. The aim is for threads of thought and insight that emerge to be viewed and extended. This process is a deliberate attempt to harness the collective initiative of the team.

Equipment: An A4 page for each person.

Process:
1. The team sits in a circle or around a large table.
2. The team leader explains that this is a search for a solution using the insights of the whole group working together.
3. The problem or situation for which a solution or strategy is needed is presented to the team. Team members may ask questions for a few minutes if they need more clarity about the matter they are deliberating.
4. Individual team members write for 5 minutes on their own sheet of paper. They are asked to apply their best thinking to the issue and write ideas, proposed solutions, aspects of the matter that should be considered, connections to other issues and so on.
5. After 5 minutes team members pass their contribution to the person on their left who is asked to:
   o Underline anything that they agree with;
   o Write connecting ideas;
   o Add to anything that is on the page;
   o Write supporting suggestions of comments;
   o Offer alternative opinions to what is written.

Or add anything that they think will build upon what is already written.
6. The pages should be circulated until each page is back with the original author who has another opportunity to build on their contribution by drawing on what has been added.
7. The pages are again passed to the next person on the left and each team member is asked to read out all of the threads on the page that have been underlined and added to. These are collected on a whiteboard.

SAILING*

SAILING is a powerful process for ensuring that all team members know what has been agreed and should be shared with all staff after the deliberations of any team, executive group or school committee. The process ensures that a proposal is carefully considered through effective consultation. The actions that are eventually taken are transparent, well-understood and will increase certainty and cohesion in the school community.

Note that the 'leader' referred to in this process does not necessarily refer to the designated leader of the team or group, but to the person who proposes a plan or actions for implementation by the team.

The **Situation** is described by the leader or agreed through dialogue in the group.

An **Action** is proposed (including a time frame)

The **Intention** of the action is explained and discussed.

The remainder of the committee or executive group actively **Listens** for understanding and may ask questions for clarification.

In small groups (2 to 4) team members share their **Interpretation** of the leader's analysis, proposal and rationale. Further questions can be asked at any time. The point of this activity is for them to fully understand and align their perceptions of the proposal.

Team members **Negotiate** their own role in the action by telling the leader:
- What believe they have heard in the proposal
- What is required of them as they take the proposal back to their own stage or team.

The negotiation is an opportunity for discussion and clarification. It must result in each team member having a clear plan of action about how to communicate the action proposed (and perhaps modified) by the leader.

Each team member commits to '**Go** for it!': to implement their action within the agreed time frame usually before the next meeting.

To maintain the sailing metaphor, each member of the exec (or committee) 'tacks' back to the people they represent, explains the proposal as clearly as possible, and then gathers feedback questions or comments from their people. If replies are contentious, the representative can use a modified SAILING process to ensure that they clearly understand what they are intended to convey to the leadership group.

At the next exec or committee meeting, responses from the groups or people who are represented are heard, discussed and a response is created, once again using SAILING if necessary.

Representatives tack back and forward until the proposal is clear and all questions or objections have been addressed – or until the exec group decide that it is time for a decision.

Note: This strategy is too elaborate to be used for routine decision-making. However, it will be time well spent when an action or initiative is proposed that will need the understanding and involvement of the whole staff.

* Based on a script by Karl Weick (as described in "The Power of Intuition", Gary Klein, Doubleday, 2004).

PERCEPTUAL POSITIONS EXERCISES

The Perceptual Positions were developed by the NLP community from pioneering work by Gregory Bateson on the different perspectives from which we can view the world.

Purpose: The purpose of these five exercises in using the Perceptual Positions is to enable the team to bring multiple perspectives to their deliberations and decisions. The quality of discussion and decision-making changes radically when team members are able to recognise their own entrenched assumptions and preferences in order to move beyond them.

Using 2nd position they can develop a more empathic understanding of the people who think differently from themselves and those who may be affected by their decisions.

Using 3rd position brings a powerful element of analytic objectivity to the team's discourse.

Applying 4th position - the leadership perspective - helps the team to adopt the big picture: to see the school as more important than their own ideology and personal preferences.

Exercise 1
1st Perceptual Position

1st Perceptual Position is self-focused. In this position we pay attention to our own thoughts, ideas and values and on our own current priorities. Having a clear understanding of our own 1st position is critical for self-awareness and self-management. It enables us to be clear about what we know and believe. It underpins the honest assertiveness that is essential to personal integrity. But however well we know ourselves, the boundaries of 1st Perceptual Position are always defined by the limitations of our own experience and the current focus of our thinking.

This Exercise is intended to identify some important 1st positions of each team member:
1. Team members work in groups of 3
2. Each team member spends a few moments in quiet reflection, identifying 3 opinions they know they hold strongly.
3. They then identify the beliefs and assumptions that underpin these opinions.
4. They share their reflections in the small group.
5. Each group shares with the whole team the opinions and related assumptions and beliefs that they consider may emerge in the team's discussions.

Exercise 2
2nd Perceptual Position

In 2nd Perceptual Position, we deliberately focus on the perceived world of other people. We do our best to think our way into the brains of others. The primary tool of 2nd Perceptual Position is listening – listening without judgment and with genuine curiosity: but it's more than listening. In 2nd position we also use our other senses to decode the messages we perceive from the total behaviour of the other person. We notice their physiology and actions, as well as listening to their words and tone of voice. As our expertise in 2nd position grows, we get a sense of what is important to the other person and why; of what things excite and discourage them' of what incidents and encounters mean through the lenses of their experience.

Using 2nd position takes effort and practice for most of us. In natural mode (1st position) we are habitually self-referencing creatures, processing whatever is said and done by other people through our own perceptual system. Whatever we hear or see, our own thoughts and interpretations flood unbidden into our consciousness, cutting off the flow of information that we receive from other people. To develop 2nd position we have to keep refocusing our attention on what we are hearing or seeing from the other person. When our own thoughts pop into our heads (as they certainly will) we have to learn to allow them to pass through our consciousness like bubbles rising to the surface of a lake, without examining them or paying any attention to them.

Exercise: This exercise provides an opportunity for team members to use 2nd position to understand a team member whilst deliberately setting aside their own thoughts and opinions.
1. Team members work in pairs.
2. Each person is asked to talk for 3 - 5 minutes about something they are passionate about. It can be work-related or personal.
3. Their partner listens in 2nd position. They can ask clarifying questions, paraphrase to check their understanding and use non-verbal encouragement cues.
4. If their own opinions or ideas bubble up in their consciousness, the listener is to deliberately ignore them (not easy – that's why second position takes effort).

Reflective questions for the whole team:
- What was most challenging about staying in 2nd position?
- As you remained focused on what you were hearing, what changed in your level of interest and appreciation?
- How would it help our deliberations if we all used this style of empathic listening?

Exercise 3

3rd Perceptual Position

Adding **3rd Perceptual Position** to our repertoire is powerful in another way. In 3rd position we attend to what is happening as if we are a detached observer simply describing what is going on. In 3rd position we can use the metaphor of a fly on the ceiling or a 'helicopter view' to explain what is happening. What we notice in 3rd Perceptual Position, is that emotion disappears (or at the least is diminished). Think how useful this can be to team. Faced with one of the many highly emotive and challenging situations in which the feelings of other people can trigger defensiveness or distress, adopting 3rd position is liberating for team members.

Exercises: These exercises encourages team members to describe situations and events with dispassionate objectivity.

1.
   a. As you sit in the team, look around at your fellow team members and describe how they seem to you as you observe them from 1st position.
   b. Next, imagine that you are observing the group from a point just below the ceiling and above the door. What can you see now? What is different about observing the team like this?
   c. See if you can move your attention to one team member at a time. What do you see?
   d. Now attend to any interactions between team members. What do you observe?

2.
   a. Think back to a disagreement or difference of opinion you have had with a colleague at some time in the past. It does not have to be recent.
   b. Working with one team-mate, describe the conflict or differences in thinking from your own point of view (1st position).
   c. Now imagine that you were an impartial observer describing the interaction between the two colleagues. In your narrative, do not mention anything that could not be seen or heard; stick to the observable features of the event.

Reflective Questions for the whole team:

- What changes in your own thoughts and feelings did you notice when you shifted into 3rd Position?
- Were you able to be impartial and objective? What did you find challenging about this?
- In what situations would it be useful for you and your team members if we all use 3rd position to describe situations which are fraught with emotions or when we are tempted to take 'sides'?

Exercise 4
4th Perceptual Position

4th Perceptual Position is the quintessential leadership viewpoint. In 4th Position, we look at the situation, the challenge, or the problem from the point of view of the organisation or team we lead. We zoom out from our own concerns and those of our colleagues to ask ourselves: "What would be best for the school?" or "What will help this school to thrive?"

The difficulty with paying attention in this way is in not giving undue weight to your own opinion. That's why the exercise asks you to consider so many ways to view the situation and the ramifications of any decision.

Exercise: use 4th perceptual position to identify the difference between what is best for you as a team member and what is best for the school. This is challenging!

1. Think of a situation where you have strong personal opinions about a particular course of action that should be taken at the school. Some examples might be:
   - how you think about the amount of time lost to extra-curricular activity;
   - your thoughts about reporting to parents;
   - your ideas about how to develop self-discipline in students.
2. Work in pairs and each asks each other at least 5 of these questions:
   - What other opinions are there about this?
   - If you were a dictator and could impose your opinions upon others, what would happen to morale among the staff?
   - Describe the prospective decision from the points of view of anyone who has a different opinion.
   - What other consideration might you have to take into account if your view was the only one considered?
   - What are the challenges related to achieving enough consensus so that everyone understands their ideas have been incorporated?
   - What decision would damage the school or inhibit students from thriving?
   - If you were looking back on this decision 10 years from now, what new perspective would that bring?

Reflective Questions:
   - How did the attempt to pay attention in 4th Position change your own thinking?
   - If the team were making a decision now, in what way will 4th Position bring different perspectives to the decision?

Exercise 5
Perceptual Agility

The practice that I describe as perceptual agility is the ability to attend to, and move between, whichever of the perceptual positions is most useful in any situation. Each of the perceptual positions is a way of paying attention to the world of experience. Each position provides an important perspective for leadership.

Exercise: This exercise enables the team to see how they can move between the perceptual positions in order to pay attention to all of the dimensions of a situation or potential decision.

1. Imagine that the team has to make a decision about any matter that is contentious in the school community. If there is a 'real' situation to consider, so much the better.

2. Team members work in groups of 4 with each team member representing a different Perceptual Position (though all 4 team members will have an opportunity to have input into all of the positions

   - Consider 1st position. What are the 1st positions held in this group?
   - Now move on to 2nd position. What other opinions and attitudes are presently held in the community?
   - In 3rd position, describe the agreements and disagreement as objectively as possible? How much division is there? Are there areas of consensus?
   - In 4th position what should be kept in mind for the school to thrive? How will this decision be portrayed if a school history was to be written in 5 years?

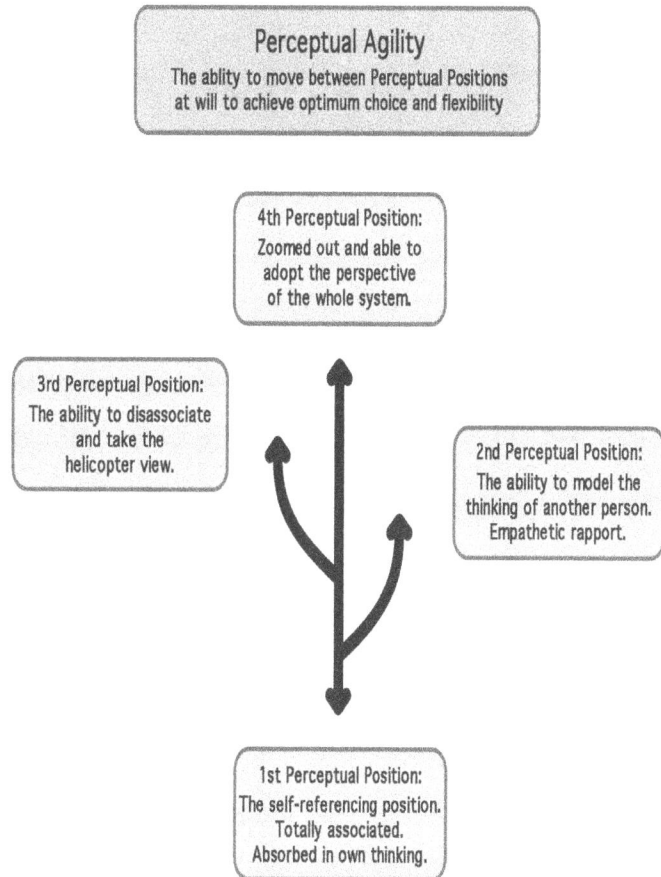

Perceptual Agility
The ability to move between Perceptual Positions at will to achieve optimum choice and flexibility

4th Perceptual Position: Zoomed out and able to adopt the perspective of the whole system.

3rd Perceptual Position: The ability to disassociate and take the helicopter view.

2nd Perceptual Position: The ability to model the thinking of another person. Empathetic rapport.

1st Perceptual Position: The self-referencing position. Totally associated. Absorbed in own thinking.

Reflection: What did perceptual agility add to the wisdom of the team?

Section Six

Team Meeting Starters

The constraints of the school day are such that meetings of the team usually take place at times that almost invite distraction:

- Before school begins when most team members are already thinking about the demands of the coming hours;
- During the school day: wedged into slivers of time between the absorbing demands of teaching and learning;
- After school when team members are already tired from the intensity of the day's activity.

These impediments often persuade team leaders that it is best to launch into the matters of the day without preamble or introduction. However, experience demonstrates that capturing the full attention of team members requires some kind of pause and refocussing: a deliberate transition between whatever has been occupying attention before the meeting and the change to more reflective mode. This means that taking 5 (or even 10) minutes to re-orient everyone into the team 'space' usually pays off.

Notes:
- The first three activities and the 'meeting check-in' are obvious 'transition' activities.
- The lists of 'Check-in' options and meeting starters offer options for brief discussions that serve the dual purpose of deepening connection between team members and ushering in the reflective mode.
- The other activities may require more time and may be more appropriate when the team gets together during staff-development days or at a team retreat.

Where's your HEAD?

Purpose: To put aside the busy-ness of life and work outside the team meeting or training activity and focus on the present moment.

Process:

1. Ask the group to stand on a socio-metric line representing their sense of how 'present' they are and how ready to focus on the team meeting or team activity.
2. *Socio-metric line:* (Place yourself on the line)

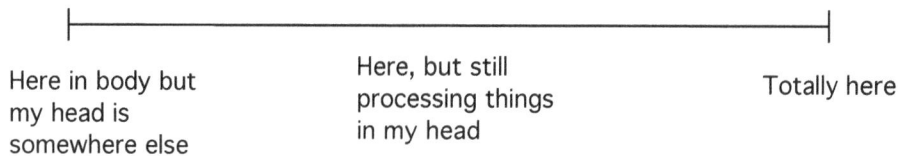

```
├────────────────────────────────────────────┤
```

Here in body but   Here, but still   Totally here
my head is   processing things
somewhere else   in my head

3. Invite group members to chat to those around them on the line about what is going on to place them at that place on the line.
4. Then ask "what will need to happen in the next 5 minutes for you to be able to (temporarily) put aside those things and become totally present in this room and the conversations we will have together.
5. Encourage sharing in the same groups and ask if more public sharing will help. What is the motivation of those who are totally here (or close) and how is that helpful to others?

Variation:
   I. Give out 'Obsessive thought' papers and ask people to write on them the things they can't let go.
   II. Ask them to place these papers in a box/on paperclips/in the custody of a colleague – then let them go for the moment.
   III. Remind them that these priorities will be there for them to collect as they leave the room.

Reflection:
The power of this activity is in acknowledging that it is difficult to bring focus to the room when there are so many other things going on AND in creating a process where participants can 'park' these priorities for the duration of the activity.

Walk and Talk Preview

Purpose:

To encourage reflective practice through collegial conversation. Can be used after or before meetings or development activity and as a regular feature of professional reflective practice.

Process:

1. Before during or after professional learning days, or as a regular feature of team or staff meetings, participants share their thinking with a professional colleague.
2. A choice of reflective partner may begin each walk and Tal. Alternatively, team members may prefer to talk with a regular reflective partner.
3. The reflective partners walk and talk for 4 to 7 minutes, sharing their recent learning or their perceptions of their day-to-day professional experience.
4. When the whole group re-convenes, participants are encouraged to share a brief insight or idea from their personal reflection with the whole group.

Reflective Activity:

- The reflection is incorporated in the activity.
- A facilitator or team leader might ask probing or observant questions as a follow-up to individual sharing if this will deepen the understanding of the individual and group.

Leave 'IT' at the Door
(collecting 'it' afterwards is optional)

Purpose:
To enable team members to put aside, for the duration of the meeting, any preoccupation, anxiety or pressing issue that is likely to distract them from the purpose of the meeting or training activity.

Equipment: A4 paper, big-nib pens. A large cardboard box.

Process:
1.	The paper and pens are available when participants enter the meeting room.

2.	Anyone who feels they have a pre-occupation or concern that they are having difficulty getting out of their head is invited to write on an A4 sheet, what it is that they need to remember; to continue thinking about; or to take action on when they leave the meeting.

3.	Participants may briefly share the concern with another persona in order to clarify the issue or anxiety before they write it down.

4.	As soon as the concern is written on the A4 paper it is placed in a very large cardboard box just inside the door.

5.	At the end of the meeting participants are reminded that they are allowed to take the A4 pages with them if they want to.

Notes:
The larger the cardboard box the better. A big box has a way of helping people put their preoccupations into perspective.
If people do not collect their 'Leave IT at the door' papers they should be shredded (It is surprising how often people do not want their papers again.

Reflective Questions:
This does not usually need further reflection - though occasionally an activity or discussion focused on the lessons learned or usefulness of this activity may be appropriate.

A Pot-Pourri of Meeting Starters
(for Connecting and Sharing)

Purpose: To enable individuals in the team to connect with other team members and share their thinking or values in some depth.

Process:
1. Use a process for pairing team members such as pairs of playing cards, coloured counters, images, etc.
2. With their partner participants are given a conversation activity which encourages personal sharing and depth of thought. Some examples are:
   - The best idea activity I have encountered in the last week;
   - Walk and talk discussing something they have learned or done as a team recently.
   - My current challenges;
   - 5 things I think my team could learn;
   - Download/Upload (share something that you want to download (get rid of) and one thing you want to find out (upload) from your partner;
   - Expert Search: who can we identify who could help us with (a team or individual problem);
   - One skill that would change my work;

The variety of conversation starters that you can use will be limited only by your imagination. Often it's good to ask team members to take turns to initiate these.

De-Brief Comments and Questions.
A debrief may not be necessary though it is sometimes useful for the team leader to ask, when he or she brings the whole group back together:
   - What were the benefits of that activity?
   - Did you find out something useful or unexpected?
   - How could those conversations help us to work well together?

Meeting Check-Ins

Purpose:
An inclusive way to begin meetings that involves everyone and enables issues to be raised and baggage left at the door. The use of 2nd perceptual position is encouraged.

Process:
Check-ins can be conducted in the whole group (in a group circle), in small groups, or during a 'walk and talk' period with one other person.

Whatever the context you choose, the following are possible check-in starters:

- o What's one thing you hope to accomplish at today's meeting?
- o Where are you getting your energy from at the moment (work or life)
- o What concern would you like to share so that you can let it go and fully concentrate on our work today?
- o What's one new and interesting thing you've been thinking about lately?
- o What kind of a day have you had so far today?
- o What's one thing that you're really proud of that you'd like to share with the group?
- o Is there a problem or concern that you would like the group to help you with?
- o Given our work so far, what do you feel best about?
- o What is the most challenging aspect of leadership in our school?
- o What have you had to put aside to come to this meeting today?
- o How can being at this meeting add value to your week?
- o What is one thing we can accomplish today that will make this time together worthwhile?
- o If you could change one thing about the last week, what would it be?
- o Which jellybean do you usually pick from the jar? (and what does it tell us about you?)
- o If you could have dinner with one world leader, whom would you invite? Why?
- o What is your best dance move? (Feel free to demo)
- o If you were to be reincarnated in another life form, what would you be and why?
- o For what in your life do you feel most grateful?
- o What would you like to do that you believe will make the world a better place??
- o What adjective best describes your personality?
- o If you could wake up tomorrow having gained any one quality or ability, what would it be?

- What colour best describes your mood today?
- What is your most important goal this month?
- If you were writing your autobiography, what would the title be?
- If you can be one of your colleagues for a day who would it be? Why?
- If you could change one thing about yourself what would that be? Why?
- What about work frustrates you the must?
- What is one thing you have learned to do, outside work, in the last 5 years?
- If you became suddenly famous, how would you avoid letting fame go to your head?

Note that you can add to these with anything that might elicit the interest and engagement of team members.

Reflection: Not usually necessary if the check-in is conducted in the whole group.

If the check in takes place in small groups or in pairs, allow an opportunity for team members to mention anything that they said or heard that they believe is significant enough for the whole group to hear.

TRUST Conversations

(Similar to page 41)

Purpose:

In the leadership context, trust is not built by accident or without thoughtful and deliberate process. This is one way of inviting team members to trust each other and share what is important to them as the meeting begins.

Process:

1. Team members are randomly selected to work together (draw names/numbers from a hat; stand in a circle then step forward and choose whoever is in your line of vision etc.)

2. Each pair takes turns to initiate a structured conversation:
    a. What is happening for you today?
    b. Is there some aspect of your role that is exciting you (or concerning you) today?
    c. What would you most like to change about how your work is going?
    d. Is there a value you would like to live up to and model for your team at the moment?

3. When the partner is answering the questions, the role of the partner is to listen with understanding.

4. At the end of each conversation, partners discuss what was most important or insightful for them in listening to the other.

Over the life of the team, all participants may be given an opportunity, over time to have a trust conversation with every other team member.

Reflective Questions.

After every trust building session the facilitator may ask:
• What was most important for you about sharing with each other?
• How did listening with understanding help to deepen your own insight about the work of leadership?
• What did you learn that you can use with your own team?

Section Seven

Team Learning: Capacity-Building and Coaching
Teams that Learn Together Grow in Capability.

One of the most significant findings of the research team led by Ruth Wageman[1] is that individual learning and personal improvement have only a limited impact on team capability. To develop the team's productivity and effectiveness, it is *team learning* that makes the greatest difference.

This has not always been the approach that school have taken to developing their teams. The culture in which individuals attend training and then report on their learning to the team is commonplace. However, that is not team learning – it is personal learning which is subsequently shared with the team and inevitably diluted in the process. Other team members only gets a 'snapshot' of the individual's learning. Although this practice is widespread, the research seems to point in a very different direction. School leaders who want to build an effective team around themselves must put aside time for team learning – occasions when the team learns together.

There are, of course, many approaches to team learning and most of these involve learning from experience. The team can learn from its successes, and from its failures; it can learn from the ways it reflects on the effects of their decisions on other people; it can learn from deliberating upon the degree of its influence and the ways that it might extend this.

A second way of learning from experience is derived from deliberate experiential learning episodes: analogous activities that imitate some of the situations the team might face. Through these, the team can take a step back from their day-to-day activity and extract some general principles which they can then apply in practice.

Both these ways of learning are enhanced by deliberate coaching. The person (or persons) responsible for coaching the team can be a member of the team, or the team leader (or even an external coach). Whichever option is chosen the process of coaching is quite deliberately focused on extending the capacity and effectiveness of the team. And the principal tool of the coach is the use of reflective questions: questions that encourage the team to self-evaluate and to continually explore new and better options together.

The activities in this section are all focused on the growth of team effectiveness, using the approaches suggested above. The activities offered here vary greatly and include:

- Activities like 'Traffic Jam' or 'Accelerator' that immerse the team in problem solving activity followed by deeply reflective thought;
- Games such as 'The Systems Game' or 'Perfect Balloon' that illustrate one or more aspects of the challenges facing leaders at all levels;
- Practices that help the team to extend and direct their influence in the school community such as the 'Story' activities and 'Circles of Influence';
- Intentionally reflective practices such as 'Learning from Experience and the 'Walk and Talk' review;
- Team coaching practices: several of which are described in detail in the last part of this chapter.

Because the life of school team members is so busy (and because team meetings can be very full of task related discussion and deliberation) this section contains much more than you will need in any one year. My intention has been to provide you with a variety of team learning activities from which to choose. Some of you may adopt team learning episodes as a regular practice, others only when they meet an emergent need.

[1]Ruth Wageman, Debra Nunes, James Burruss and Richard Hackman: *'Senior Leadership Teams'* 2008.

The Token Game

Purpose:
To demonstrate that CHOICE is the basis of human behaviour and motivation.
This is always a useful reminder for the team. The staff they lead - or work with – are internally controlled: they make their own choices.

Equipment: Several dozen small plastic tokens

Process:
1. The team leader or facilitator distributes coloured plastic tokens among the participants: Some get no tokens; others receive various quantities and variations of colour.
2. Each person is asked to set themselves a goal: A specific number and specific colours of tokens they wish to obtain during the 5 minutes of the activity.
3. Participants are told that they can use any strategy **except** physical violence to obtain what they want.
4. After 5 minutes participants are asked to show what they have obtained and whether they achieved their goal?
5. Each person also describes how they went about achieving their goal.

Reflective Questions and Comment:
- Whatever you ended up with, who made the choice to either keep, trade, or hand over the token(s)?
- Why was there such variation in what team members decided to collect and why they had such different goals?
- Was it possible (without violence) to get a token that another person did not want to give up?
- Were all of the strategies used to obtain tokens ethical and likely to improve or maintain a relationship?
- How is this understanding of human will and motivation useful to us in our work with our colleagues - as well as with students?

Walk and Talk Review

Purpose:
To encourage reflective practice through collegial conversation. Can be used after or before meetings, events or training - or as a regular feature of professional reflective practice.

Equipment: none. (A reflective diary and coloured pens for the 'Hatswell variation').

Process:
1. Before during or after professional activity or meetings (or as a regular feature of staff or leadership meetings) participants share their thinking with a professional colleague.
2. Reflective partners may be chosen for the session, the course, in the participants school location or chosen at a moment in time.
3. The reflective partners walk and talk for 6 to 8 minutes, sharing their recent learning or their perceptions of their day-to-day professional experience.
4. When the whole group re-convenes, participants are encouraged to share the insights and ideas from their personal reflection with the whole group.

Variations:
5. The Judy Hatswell variation:

Judy uses a more structured version of this process.
- First reflective partners walk and talk.
- Then individuals capture their own reflection in a reflective diary using colour and images to illustrate their thinking.
- Then they share in small groups before a whole group sharing session is conducted.

Reflective Questions:

- The reflection is incorporated in the activity.
- A facilitator or coach might ask probing or observant questions to deepen the understanding of the individual and group.

The Systems Game

I learned this activity from the website *businessballs.com*

Purpose: To illustrate the complexity of human interaction by setting up the simplest possible system (2 moving parts). The activity also shows that systems can be deliberately influenced but conversely that they easily produce unexpected and unwanted consequences. It also demonstrates that in a human system of any kind, people follow significant people but are blind to whoever is following them as well as having little understanding of who their colleagues are following.

Process: At least 12-15 people are needed for this activity.

1. Participants stand in a large open space- preferably outdoors. They form a circle to begin with.
2. Two instructions are given. The first is: 'Select two other people as your 'markers' without indicating who it is you have chosen'. The second is: 'When the game starts, move so as to keep an equal distance between you and each of these two people at all times.' (i.e. create an equilateral triangle).
3. When the instruction to begin is given, participants immediately begin to move to position themselves as instructed, each movement triggering many others. The process sometimes speeds up for a while, at times slow down toward equilibrium, but if everyone is trying to maintain an exact equilateral triangle between themselves and their markers it should never stop completely.
4. At some point a section of the group can be asked to take on a second agenda such as moving in a particular direction as they adjust their position (they must still remain true to the 'equilateral triangle 'agenda).

Reflective questions:
- What did we learn?
- You were very aware of the two markers you were following. Dd you know who was following you? Did you notice anyone else who was following your markers? What does that illustrate about our perception of who is influential in our school?
- What does the activity illustrate about the characteristics of a 'self-organising' system? What systems in our school are 'self-organising' ?
- How do we impose intention on such a system?

Circles of Influence
(*A strategy for mapping influence - developed by Rob Stones and Deborah Ward*)

Purpose: To prepare a simple representation of the spread of influence the team has across the school and to initiate planning to extend that influence as required.

Process:

1. This activity is most powerful when the circles of influence are presented in the language of the group, so the initial step is to ask the group to give you a list of all the types and subjects of conversation and interaction that can be heard in the workplace.

2. As these are shared with you, list them on one side of the whiteboard, and categorise them in four groups, separated by horizontal lines:

   o In the top group, place anything that is about values, beliefs, and informs others about who you are, and what you are passionate about, when you are being the best you can be.

   o In the middle group, place conversations that are task oriented, strategic or goal related. Information about what is to be done and discussions about how it might best be achieved.

   o In the third group put operational, factual and procedural matters

   o In the bottom section, identify interactions that are commands, instructions, detailed information about how things should be done, procedures and system expectations.

   Note that 'gossip' will always come up at some stage. Write it on the other side of the whiteboard and leave it there for the present.

3. Label the top group the 'values'. Label the middle group Tasks and Goals'. Label the next group 'procedures or operations'. Label the bottom group ''Expectations and instructions' – once again adapt these if necessary to the language of the group.

4. Now draw 4 concentric circles on the whiteboard. In the inner circle write: 'many values conversations'. In the next one: 'tasks, goals and strategy' – this might include occasional *one-to-one*

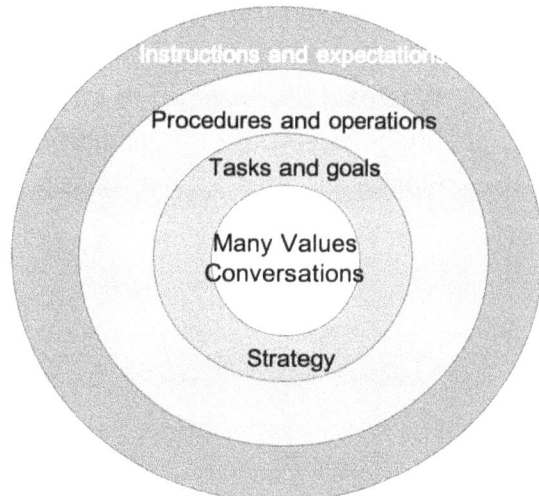

Concentric circles, from outer to inner: Instructions and expectations; Procedures and operations; Tasks and goals; Many Values Conversations; Strategy

values conversations. In the third circle: 'mostly operations and procedures' (values only in formal settings such as meetings). In the outer circle: 'instructions and expectations'.

5. Ask the group to write, in each circle, where all the people that they work with belong (if it is a very large organisation, suggest that they sample). Emphasise that this will be private and though they may want to share their personal circles later in the activity, they will not have to do so!!

6. Ask the group individually to analyse the contents of their circles.
   o Where have they placed the people whom they influence the most and who are most influential with them? (Invariably it will be in the inner circles).
   o Where are the people who are most difficult to manage? Who do they feel they have little influence over (though they may have positional power over them), and who comply grudgingly, or passively resist?
   o If we define influence as 'the effect we have on people as a result of establishing 'vulnerability-based trust' how would team members describe their spread of influence within the staff?
   o Does this analysis suggest that the team should take some action?

Debriefing questions:
   o How might the team bring 'difficult' people into the inner rings?
   o How important is it to this team to increase the spread of their effective influence?
   o What should the team do about 'outliers' – those who are in the outer circles of everyone in the team?
   o What can the team do to strategically reduce those in the outer circles and to bring more staff or community members into the inner 2 circles?
   o Finally, ask them to put 'gossip' into the circles. How does it work?

Traffic Jam

Purpose:

To explore some of the challenges facing every team:

- Paradigm blindness;
- Not thinking through the consequences of actions;
- Not seeing the need to involve all team members in learning and change.

Equipment: Hoops or overturned chairs

Process:

The traffic 'route' is set up using hoops, or by turning chairs on their back so that the space between the legs creates the slots. Set up the traffic route so that there is one more space than there are participating team members.

In the following description the team has 12 members, split into two sub-groups of 6. (Note, numbers must be even – if an extra person they can observe or coach. It helps if the sides can be distinguished in some way: e.g. dark clothing/light clothing)

The traffic route looks like this when set up (note the space is between the 2 sides):

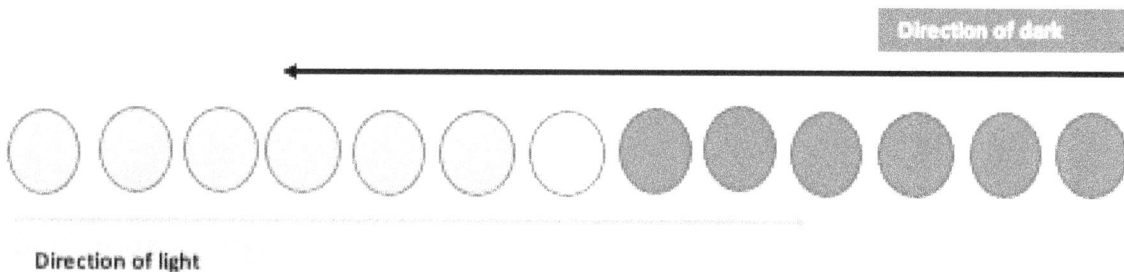

Direction of dark

Direction of light

The aim of the activity is for each side to move all of its members to the other end of the traffic route using only two kinds of moves:

1. Step forward into an empty slot in front of you:
2. Jump the person in front of you into an empty slot beyond them.
- NO other moves are possible.
- If the sides get stuck they must start again from the beginning

This is how the sides aim to finish up:

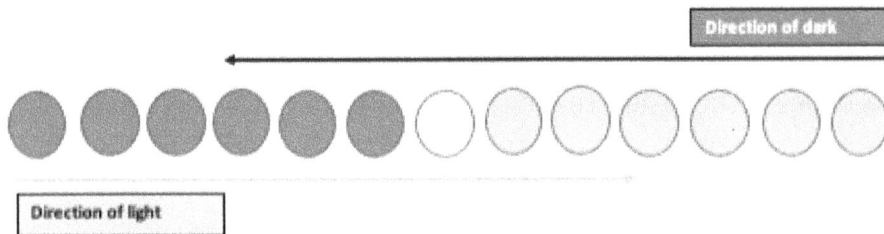

Occasionally someone with good visualisation skills will immediately be able to see how to proceed. This rarely happens. The most common scenario is that sides keep making forward moves that block their progress.

As the facilitator, it's OK to give question clues because they all help the de-brief at the end. The two most common clues I offer is:
- Can you identify what blocks you?
- What moves can you make to avoid what keeps blocking you?

If there is time, when the sides have found and implemented the solution, ask them to turn around and repeat the activity, now with different people at the front (decision-making end) of each sub-team. It's often the case that these people will not know what to do because the 'action' has been so far from them the first time through.

Reflective Questions

Debrief for:

1. Paradigm blindness: when you are locked in the 'who moves next paradigm' the problem looks unsolvable. When you shift to the 'avoiding what is blocking us' paradigm, the solution is quickly found.
    a. Ask - what paradigms are we locked into in our team?
    b. What other ways of seeing our blockers could there be?

2. Linear thinking: only looking for the next step. Good leadership decisions almost always benefit from anticipating the consequences of our decisions – or even better, searching for the consequences of the consequences of every decision.

    Ask – How can we make sure we are leaders who act like competent chess players: always looking beyond the next move and the next and anticipating the consequences of this chain of action?

3. The danger of the inner circle. In schools decisions about change or progress are often made by an inner circle – the exec team or a 'committee'. This 'inner circle' wrestles with the complexities of the problem they are solving in order to craft a way forward. It's unrealistic to expect those on the outer to have the same understanding and commitment as the inner circle unless they are invited to the same level of thinking.

Ask – how do we ensure that the staff are not only told 'what to do' but are also invited to engage with the 'why' of the change initiative.

The Learning Triangle

Purpose: To identify the kind of learning events that are preferred by team members. This is important knowledge for a team which will be committed to learning together. It enables the team leader and team members to design and present information and experiences in a way that will appeal to everyone.

Equipment: Room to spread out. 3 Markers or Chairs to form a triangle.

Process:
1. The team leader or whoever is leading the activity marks out an equilateral triangle in the room, with each of the three vertices representing a preference for a type of learning:
   - 'Head' learning. Knowledge and understanding are most important. Reasons are critical – Why the learning is needed – 'Why should we do this?'
   - 'Hands' learning. Practical and transactional activity is preferred. Experiential learning and a clear emphasis on HOW. Skills and ability are valued, and action is the emphasis - 'What will I actually DO?'
   - 'Heart' Learning. Values and beliefs are the drivers of learning. What will this mean for us, how will we change as a result. What will make things better? 'How will our lives improve as a result?'
2. Team members stand at the point which represent the type of learning they need - or feel most comfortable with.
3. With the group at their vertex they discuss the best way to describe what they need to engage them in learning and to learn effectively **and** what discourages them from learning.
4. Each group then presents their learning preference and dislike to the whole team.
5. Team members stand in a place on the triangle which indicates their 2nd preference as well as their first.
6. The group discusses the significance of this second preference.

Reflective Questions:
- What have we learned about how (or how not) to engage the learning of the group?
- How will we use this knowledge?

Learning from Experience

Purpose: To help members of the team put their team learning into practice

Process:

1. Team members are asked to identify two or three days in each term when they will record their use of the 'ideal' leadership behaviours that have been the subject of team learning and discussion.
2. On each identified day, participants should record any activity or conversation (either positive or negative) that relates to the leadership behaviours that have been promoted in the team context.
3. Each action or conversation they note should be followed by a reflective statement that answers two questions:
   a. 'How did I feel about my action or behaviour?'
   b. 'How does my action or behaviour align with what we have identified as leadership best practice?'
4. Following the identified days the team puts aside time to discuss the results of their actions and reflections. Team members work with a partner they trust enough to be completely open with and share what they did and their post-action reflection.
5. A whole group discussion invites sharing from each pair of team members.

Reflective questions:

- What did you discover about putting 'ideal' leadership behaviours into practice?
- What will you do in the future as a result of this activity and reflection?
- Are there some learnings for the team that are suggested by your experience?
- How can this experience help us to conduct team learning that is even more relevant and useful?

Accelerator

Purpose: To initiate discussion on what 'continuous improvement of our professional practice' means .

Equipment: one soft ball or beanbag for every group of 4 to 5 team members.

Process:
1. Team members stand in groups of 4 to 5 (you can be flexible about this especially if you only have a small team. However, less than 4 does not work so well).
2. Team members stand at arms-length (about 1.5 metres) from each other in a 'circle' and pass the ball around the circle in a clockwise direction. The ball must leave the hand of the person who is passing it before it is grasped by the next person.
3. The aim is to pass the ball around the circle 5 times - as speedily and as smoothly as possible.
4. After an initial practice attempt, teams are asked to improve their speed and performance in any way they can (but without getting any closer to each other). If there are several groups they will almost certainly 'compete' to be the best. If there is only one group they can compete against the clock.
5. Allow the groups several attempts to improve their performance, with some discussion and planning between each attempt.

Reflective questions:
(Note that the first 5 can be asked as the activity develops, not only at the end).
- Which is most important for improvement: skill or speed?
- What else is a factor in performance improvement?
- Is there a point where trying to improve speed inhibits other aspects of performance?
- How much of a factor was planning / team communication in performance improvement?
- In what way did feeling under pressure affect performance?
- What can we extract from this activity that is relevant to our 'continuous improvement' of professional practice?
- Are there any principles we can derive from the activity that could help us guide either our own improvement or our attempts to encourage improved performance in teachers or students?

Rope Knots

Purpose: This activity is a light-hearted way of illustrating the coordination and support that team members can give each other to solve a problem.

Equipment: A length of rope that is 1 metre long for each member of the team. An overhand knot is tied in the rope every metre of its length.

Process:
1. Team members grasp the rope with one hand either side of a knot. They then let go with their right hand so that they are holding on with only their left hand.
2. When the instruction to begin is given, the team must work out how to undo every knot in the rope without letting go of the rope with their left hand.
3. The team should work from both ends of the rope at once.
4. The activity continues until the last knot is untied.

An extension activity (for those who like a challenge) would be for team members to keep hold of the rope with their left hand and re-tie every knot!

Reflective Questions:
- What were the key factors in successfully undoing every knot?
- Did every team member remain involved all of the time?
- Did some team members take the lead and others follow?
- What did 'followers' need to do to assist the leaders?
- Did one end of the rope work out what to do more quickly than the other?
- Did both ends work together or did a 'competition' emerge?
- What can we learn from this activity about ways to work together to solve both team problems and problems that confront individual members of the team?

The PERFECT Balloon

Purpose: An activity that reminds team members of the importance of giving transparent and unambiguous information and direction to the people that they lead and work with.

Equipment: A plentiful supply of balloons. A pin for the 'boss'.

Process:
- The team is broken into groups of two or three. Each group works independently.
- The 'boss' decides, without telling anyone, what the perfect balloon will be. He or she should decide on an unlikely size, perhaps tied off in a strange way and presented with some kind of elaborate action.
- The 'boss' gives this instruction to the groups:
  > 'Your job is to present the PERFECT balloon to me. It must be inflated to the correct size, tied off correctly and given to me in exactly the right way. I expect you to gather the clues about what constitutes the PERFECT balloon from prior knowledge and careful observation.'
- The groups discuss what they think is expected or intended and when they are ready, one group member presents their version of the 'perfect balloon' to the 'boss'. Unless the balloon matches the predetermined perfection visualised by the 'boss' he or she burst it with the pin. The 'boss' should not say anything and as far as possible keep an expressionless face!
- The groups will become increasingly frustrated with their 'boss' (and may even rebel completely) but the 'boss' should keep urging them to persist and may even provoke the groups by wondering aloud why they are so inept!
- The activity ends when either a group manages to guess correctly what the 'boss' wants, or when everyone is too frustrated to continue.

Reflective questions:
- What was the point of this activity?
- Have any of us felt that kind of frustration in our working lives?
- As teachers and leaders, what does this activity have to say about the importance of letting our students or colleagues know exactly what we want from them?
- We know that everything that any of us wants has to be processed through two perceptual systems: our own and the person we are communicating with. What can go wrong? How can we maximise the chance that what we intend is what is perceived?

STORY Cards

The activity was introduced to me by Judy Hatswell and originally developed by Dr Ali Sahebi.

Purpose:

To practise and experiment with the creation of stories that illustrate something of significance. Because 'story' creation and delivery is an important influencing practice, this is always a useful development activity for the team.

Equipment: Story cards. See Appendix 1 (page 207-211) for a Story-Card Resource that you can copy and cut up into 45 cards.

Process:

1. Participants form concentric circles with those in the outer ring paired with - and facing - a partner in the inner ring.
2. The facilitator explains that creating effective stories to use as examples and metaphors is an important skill for leaders.
3. Those in the outer ring are given a story card containing some words and phrases. They have 1 minute to create the most meaningful story possible to match the 'content' on their card. After the 1-minute preparation they tell their story.
4. The person hearing the story thanks the story-teller (if they want to they can say what the story meant to them).
5. The outer ring moves clockwise one position and this time it is the person on the inner ring who receives the card and creates a story for their new partner.
6. After these stories are told the person on the outer ring responds and the inner ring moves one place anti-clockwise.
7. Continue for 3 to 5 rounds.

Reflective Questions and Activity:

- 'It is said that story cuts through to deep levels of meaning, bypassing the critical or analytic habit that we bring to facts'.
  How does this correspond to your experience of hearing meaningful stories?
- What are the stories that you need to tell in order to communicate deep levels of meaning to our colleagues?
- Work in small groups to co-create stories that will be useful to one or all of the team.

What Stories Do You Want Told?

Purpose:
To design and create the narratives which will be most helpful to the team's leadership - and to the culture team members want to create.

Process:
1. Participants work in pairs and small groups to discuss the stories that they would like to hear told about themselves (or the team) and the leadership culture they would like to create (the way we do things around here!)
2. An example is offered: A Principal who wanted to change his school from a rule-governed organisation to one in which creativity was valued, took 2 actions to convince the staff that he was serious:
   - He asked his staff to bring their weighty procedures manuals to a meeting in the courtyard. When they got there, he had a bonfire burning. He invited everyone to take out any pages in the manual that limited their personal creativity and ingenuity and add these pages to the bonfire. [Most got into the spirit and burned many of their pages].
   - He gave everyone 'free mis-take' tokens to cash in when they tried something with positive intent that failed spectacularly.
3. Team members discuss the example and what it illustrates to them. Whoever is presenting the activity might like to suggest that 'what we do as a team will speak for us more clearly than what we say'
4. In pairs or groups, the participants then discuss:
   - The stories they would like to hear about themselves as individual leaders;
   - The narratives they would like to hear about the team and the way the school is served by their effectiveness.
   - The events, actions, activities or conversations that are likely to generate the stories they want to be told
3. Each participant designs and describes at least one story-worthy action they will take in the next week. The group workshops the plan of each group member to refine or modify the intended actions AND to identify any unintended consequences and how they might be avoided.

Reflective Questions and Activity:
- What were the most challenging and most useful aspects of this activity?
- How would your leadership change if you were to choose your words and actions with an eye on to their effect on culture and the stories about the way we do things around here?
- List the stories that you do **not** want to hear told. Then create ideas for events or actions that will challenge the perceptions generating those stories.

Team Maze Activity
(As taught to me by Judy Hatswell)

Equipment: A maze as illustrated below. A BEEP sound producer.

Purpose:
To create and examine some aspects of effective teamwork through finding the correct pattern through the maze.

Process:

1. A large maze is constructed, either on a sheet of material or by locating coloured circles as per the diagram below. Each row is a different colour except the first and last rows which are black. The facilitator alone knows the pattern, which does not change. Participants work as one team who are asked to work together (effective maximum 12 to 15 per maze)

2. After a 5-minute planning period, team members enter the maze one at a time. Each team member builds on the pattern discovered by those who go before them.

3. Once the first person has entered the maze participants may not talk or write anything down. They may communicate by sign. All team members must take their turn in rotation.

4. As each team member enters the maze, the facilitator gives a 'thumb up' signal if on the right path, a BEEP signal if they are wrong.

5. When a team member receives a BEEP, they must retrace their steps along the path they have travelled so far before the next team member can enter the maze.

6. The objective is to have all team members successfully traverse the maze on the correct path.

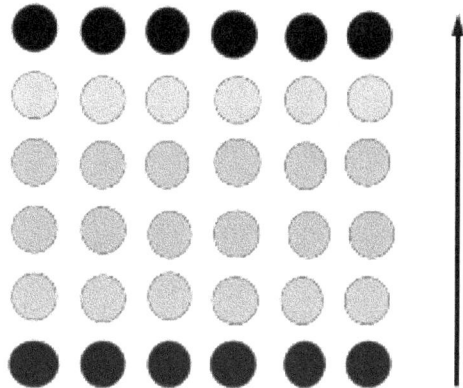

Reflective Questions:

- What elements of effective teamwork did you discover as you worked together on the maze problem?
- What was helpful and what was unhelpful for you when you were on the maze?
- How useful was your initial plan when you began to work in the maze?
- What can we learn from this activity to enhance our own team performance?

Wrecktangles

Purpose: To provide an exercise in self-management and patient persistence. The activity is also a good follow up for learning about team-work and support for others.

Equipment: Large and complex tangrams cut from 60cm x 60cm card. Each tangram should have at least 22 pieces but be made up of 4 x 30cm x 30cm squares (though the pieces should be cut in a way that obscures this).

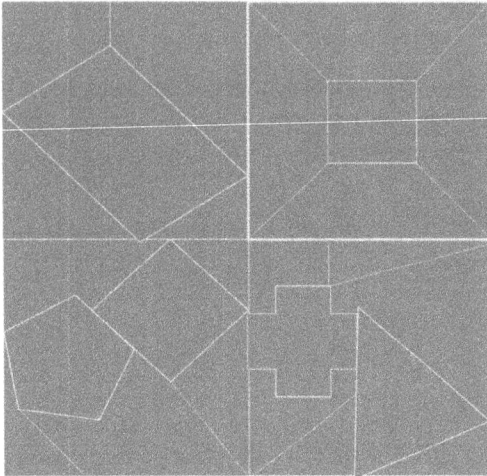

E.g.: Ideally, each tangram should be different. Try to construct the different tangrams so that at least one is relatively straightforward, at least one is quite difficult. There should be enough tangrams so that each group of 3-5 participants can work on their own puzzle.

Process:
1. The Tangrams are broken up into their parts laid on tables large enough for the tangrams to be assembled. Participants are grouped so that there are no more than 3-5 people per tangram.
2. The facilitator says' the aim is for all of the tangrams to be assembled in the shortest possible time.
3. Participants begin work on their puzzles. Almost everyone will begin with enthusiasm, but the facilitator will notice that some quickly become bored and show signs that they don't believe in their ability to solve the puzzle.
4. Inevitably, groups finish at different times, especially if some puzzles are more difficult than others. The facilitator will notice that some of the early finishers behave as if their task is done, others move off to observe or help other groups.
5. If people move from their own puzzle to help others the facilitator can encourage this.
6. Keep the activity going until the last group has finished (even though this can be frustrating for participants. (The activity works best when it is at the end of the day!)

Debrief: This activity is rich in debriefing opportunities. The facilitator can often initiate his or her questions by pointing out what they observed in the behaviour of participants though **never naming any particular person**.

Questions can relate to:
- The difficulty of managing self when the task was frustrating.
- The temptation to hang back and leave the responsibility of finishing the puzzle to other people.
- The temptation to regard the activity as a competition.
- The behaviours noticed by the facilitator.
- Whether or not the participants saw themselves as responsible for the whole task or just their own puzzle.
- The way that this activity relates to attitudes and activity within their own team.

Unblind Square

Equipment: a long rope at least 1.5 metres per participant, 1 blindfold per person, 4 x A3 paper each with one of the following shapes displayed:

Purpose:
To demonstrate that team outcomes are minimal when team members depend upon the leader for direction. Can be used to illustrate the 'Paradox of Power' and the dependence of the leader.

Process:
1. A rope, joined at the ends, is laid on the floor in a rough circle.
2. A team leader is chosen.
3. Everyone stands outside the circle. Everyone except the team leader picks up the rope and puts on their blindfolds
4. The team leader is shown the picture of the square and asked to create that shape with the rope. The usual result is that the nominated leader completes this task by micromanaging each person's position, moving them about by instructions or often physically.
5. When the leader is satisfied, the rope is placed on the ground, blindfolds removed, and the facilitator asks any of the appropriate the debriefing questions (below).
6. After the de-brief a new leader is chosen or volunteers. A new shape is chosen (the triangle or the double triangle) and the exercise is repeated. Usually (having listened to the debrief) the leader gives more information but usually creates the shape in a similar way to the first leader.
7. The facilitator conducts a second de-brief asking question ii as well as question I.
8. A fresh leader is again chosen but this time the group are not blindfolded. All are shown the 5-pointed star shape.
9. When the shape has been created the Facilitator asks all 5 of the debriefing questions:

Reflective Questions.
i. What was most effective in creating the shape? what were your feelings during the activity? How much ownership of the outcome did you have?
ii. What changes when everyone can see and knows what shape to create?
iii. Were there any new complications for the team once everyone can see what to do?
iv. How does the leader's role change when everyone can 'see'?
v. What does this activity illustrate about effective leadership?

Zoom Perspective
(Created by Istvan Banyai)

Equipment: A copy of the ZOOM picture narrative created by Istvan Banyai. You can purchase and download this series of 31 pictures from the net (either as a book or a slide show) and print them for the activity.

Purpose: - To give the team an experience of changing the frame size of any experience in order to acquire a deeper understanding of 'big picture' thinking and 'zooming out'.
- To help the team acquire perspective on any of the issues that it is dealing with.

Process:
1. Randomly distribute the 31 pictures among team members.
2. Ask the team to work together to assemble the pictures in the order of the 'story' that is told by the series.
3. Allow time for discussion about the significance of the activity.

Debriefing questions:
- Can we think of ways in which the degree of ZOOM makes a difference to the way we look at any of the issues that are the responsibility of this team?
- How might we ZOOM out to get a different perspective on any of these situations:
  - A student who is finding it difficult to learn to read.
  - A teacher who is not willing to extend their repertoire of practice.
  - A student who says they hate school.
  (you can make up your own scenarios to fit your context.)
- When is it appropriate to zoom in and ask questions that lead to greater specificity? The key question is 'What specifically?'.
- When is it best to zoom out and ask questions about what the current subject is an example of? The key question: 'What is this an example of?'.

Blind Ball Toss

Equipment: 2 balls for each person - juggling balls or 'cush' balls are ideal. An outdoor space or large room.

Purpose: To practice group/team co-ordination and communication.

Process:
- Work in groups of 4 to 6.
- In each group, one person is nominated as the 'launcher'. The 'launcher' is blindfolded and faces away from the other members of the group who must stand at least 3 metres behind the 'launcher'.

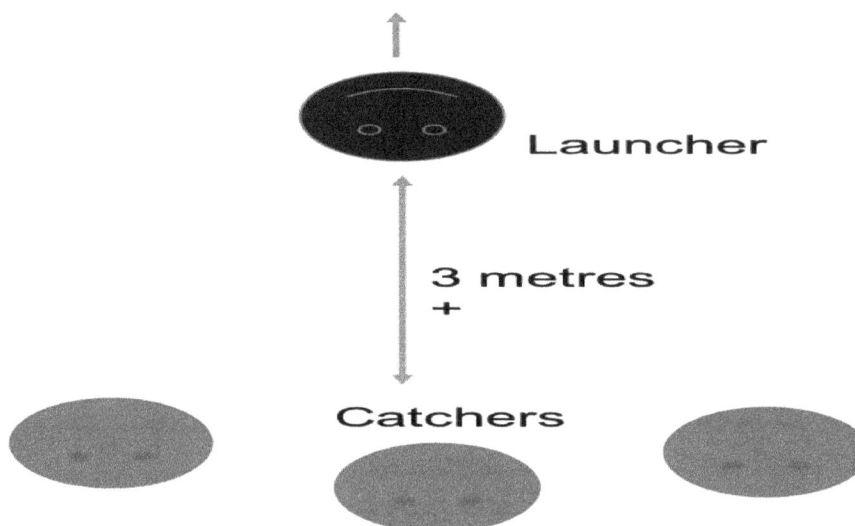

Launcher

3 metres +

Catchers

- The 'launcher' tosses the balls over their shoulder, one at a time. The job of each group member is to catch two balls each. Balls that are not caught (i.e. hit the ground) are placed back at the feet of the 'launcher'.
- The catchers must give the 'launcher' as much information as possible about where and how they want the ball launched.
- Any catcher who has successfully held two balls must retire leaving the remaining catchers to deal with any remaining tosses. The activity continues until all balls have been successfully caught.
- Once all balls have been caught change the launcher and continue as before.
- When everyone has been the launcher and all balls are caught the activity is complete.
- The activity can be competitive if there are several groups of equal size.

- Many variations are possible and can be left to the imagination of the facilitator.

Reflective Questions:

2. What did group members learn about communication and teamwork?
3. In what ways did group members use the most able catcher(s) and support those who have a lower standard of coordination?
4. How does this activity shed light on the way team members can work together even more effectively?

Pass the Stone

Equipment: Two small stones – one for each half of the team.

Purpose: to tune awareness of non-verbal communication

Process
Team members sit or stand in two equal lines facing each other. The end person is given a small stone to be passed down the line. When told to start, both teams keep their hands in front of them and carefully pass the stone down the line while keeping their stone concealed from team members in the opposite line. At any point, a team member can pretend to pass the stone but keep it in their hand. The remainder of the people in their line still act out 'passing' the stone.

When the last person in each line appears to have received the stone, the opposing line must huddle together decide where the stone really is AND (if they are correct) name the non-verbal cues that they used in making their decision.

Debrief:
Finish the activity with some questions that promote a discussion about non-verbal communication and its importance in our profession.
- What do we notice that helps us to interpret what another person is really doing?
- How do we discern another person's intention? (or is that impossible?)
- What proportion of all communication is non-verbal?
- Why is that significant for those in this team and for educators in general?

Coaching the Team

Purpose: Coaching the team can make a significant difference to team effectiveness. Without a coach (or coaches) the team can easily get so engrossed in the multitude of team tasks that they forget to stop and evaluate: "How well are we performing?" or "How can we be even more effective?"

If there is a nominated team coach their job is always to be thinking about the way the team is functioning and how to improve its effectiveness. The coach can be the team leader or a team member (or group of team members) who takes on this responsibility. Occasionally the coach may be someone who is specially added to the team for that purpose.

There are three requirements for a team coach, whoever they are:
1. They must be trusted by the team;
2. They must be thoughtful observers of team process and interaction - habitually using 3rd Perceptual Position; (It's sometimes not easy to be a team member and an observer).
3. Their job is almost always to ask questions rather than make judgments. An effective coach is an expert question-asker. The debriefing questions at the end of most activities in this book are grist for the coaches mill!

Coaching processes:
I suggest FOUR ways in which the coach can work with the team:
1. The principal mode is **reflective questioning** – helping the team learn though refection and self-evaluation.
2. A second mode is to offer the team an **Analytic Observation** from **3rd Perceptual Position**. Observations are best when embedded in (or followed by) a question, such as "Do you think that we might be stating our own positions without listening to each other's viewpoints?" or "Are we getting stuck over a difference in our beliefs (or our understanding of purpose) in this conversation?"
3. A third method is to use the **'Reality Thinking'** or **'WDEOP' coaching** process to help the team to work through a particular issue or to review their options (see below).
4. A fourth mode involves asking the team to make a **comparison with their explicit norms** or their 'Window of Certainty' as a standard against which to judge their deliberations and decisions. Once again, this intervention would usually be in the form of questions.

More detail about each of these approaches to coaching the team is offered below:

1. **Reflective Questions (or After-Action Reflection)**

   When any decision has been reached by the team, or any action taken as a result of team deliberation, the team learns by asking itself:
   - 'Have we got it right?'
   - 'Could we have done better?'

   Occasionally those questions may be asked immediately. Most often the appropriate time for this reflection will be days or weeks afterwards when the effects of the team's choices and the responses of the people affected are known.

   Whether the team's decisions were the best possible or not, the purpose of this reflection is LEARNING. It's not about agonising over an imperfect choice or actions: certainly not about justifying the option taken. The whole point of this reflection is for the team to calibrate its future decisions and deeds based on thoughtful examination of what was learned from the past.

   Other After-Action Questions might be:
   - 'What did we intend?' – 'What actually happened?' – 'What can we learn from that?'
   - 'Were there some ways we implemented or communicated the purpose of our decision that could be improved?'

2. **Analytic Observer (3rd Perceptual Position)**

   In this mode, the coach deliberately uses 3rd Perceptual Position as they observe and listen to the way that the team is working together. Whenever they feel it will be useful they offer a 3rd position. Observation that will help the team gain a greater understanding of their own processes and behaviours.

   The observations made by the coach should be analytic, but neutral – offering no hint of criticism in voice or tone. This is most easily achieved if the observation is embedded in a question or in a metaphor. Some examples might be:
   - 'Does it seem to everyone that we are going around in circles?'
   - 'Is there some polarisation of views happening as we discuss this?'
   - 'There seems to be a lot of passion in this discussion at present. Would we be able to sort through the issues more easily if we took the heat out of the interchanges?'
   - 'Can I summarise what I am hearing in this discussion?'

3. Coaching using Reality Thinking (WDEOP).

When it will be helpful to frame a discussion around the goal that the team wants to achieve, the coach can use the 'Reality Thinking or WDEOP process - referred to in the "Decision-Making' section of this manual.

The advantage of this process, especially when it is applied to recurrent issues where past actions by the team are not perceived as effective, is that it helps the team:

- Achieve clarity about their goal;
- Evaluate past decisions and actions;
- Frame and commit to fresh options or solutions.

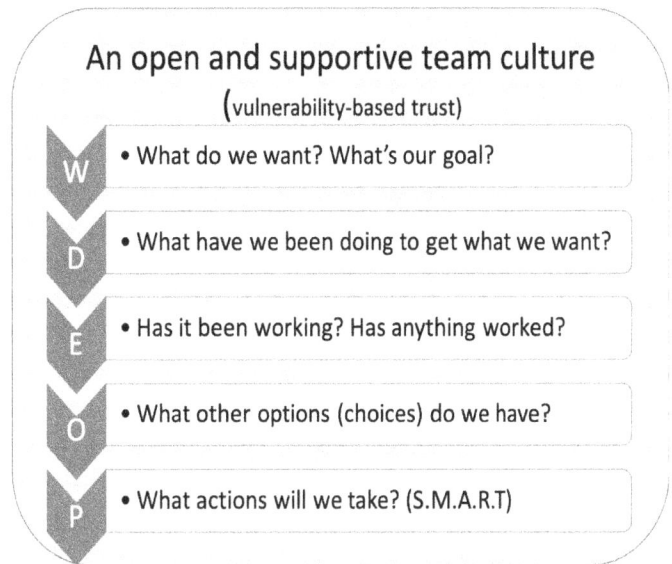

An open and supportive team culture
(vulnerability-based trust)

W	• What do we want? What's our goal?
D	• What have we been doing to get what we want?
E	• Has it been working? Has anything worked?
O	• What other options (choices) do we have?
P	• What actions will we take? (S.M.A.R.T)

In this mode the coach is more actively guiding the team than when employing the previous approaches. However, the focus for the coach is on following the steps of the procedure, not on advocating a particular course of action. The coach's guidance is procedural – it is still the team that will be guided to make the decision.

4. Comparing with Team Norms or Purpose

This method is important when the team appears to be drifting away from the Norms they have set themselves or the 'Window of Certainty' they have constructed.

It's not unusual for a team to get a little lost in its own discussions; to forget its own procedural norms or agreed purpose as a team; or even to forget the beliefs and values they agreed should frame every decision by the team.

In these circumstances, the work of the coach will be to gently but firmly draw the team back to the guiding principles they have set for themselves. Questions such as:

- Are we sticking to our norm about participating fully/asking questions about anything that is not clear?
- Is what has been proposed in alignment with our shared belief about the importance of trust and good relationships?

- Does this way of communicating the decision fit with our chosen value-in-action related to respectful consultation?

Finally a few general points about team coaching:

1. **The emphasis is on the whole team working together.** While it may also be useful and appropriate for individuals to receive coaching and for negotiation and mediation between team members to be conducted, these are not the priority. The critical goal of the team coach is to enhance the effectiveness of the team as a whole.

2. **There is no formula** for team effectiveness. As discussed in the opening pages of this manual, teams form; explore each other's diverse strengths; create norms and frameworks that help them function well; and then perform in unique ways. The job of the coach is to learn how **this** team will work best and help **these** team members to discover how to be most effective with each other.

3. Coaching a team requires some **systems thinking**. The coach must always be thinking a few steps ahead: what will be the consequences (intended or unintended) of working in a particular way - or of a particular decision. Linear solutions, without consideration of their implications or consequences should always be treated with suspicion!

4. **The Coach should take a long-term view** and encourage the team to do the same. Coaching the team isn't likely to have immediate results. If a team coach is persistent and patient, working within the trust boundaries of the team, both the team and the individuals within it will learn more effectively.

Section Eight

26 Team Energisers

Energising activity is a much-neglected feature of team practice. After all, who would not want to inject vitality, animation, exuberance and enjoyment into the activity of their team? Energisers also increase connection between team members; switch on the enthusiasm of the team, elevate the mood of team meetings - and can quite often become an opportunity for meaningful team learning.

You can use energisers to introduce a learning episode; to aid concentration during a long dry meeting or presentation; as an alternative to a meeting starter; or simply to help the team have fun together in a constructive way.

The 26 energising activities listed here are very varied. Some are very active, some quite competitive, some more relaxing and reflective. Most need no equipment. For the rest a few soft balls, a rope, some scarves and a handful of tokens will suffice.

The majority of these energisers also illustrate one or another aspect of team performance or leadership, so they can be used for team development as well as for enjoyment and vigour. In particular 'The Jedi Mind Game', 'Change the Wheels', 'Dragon Tails', and 'Improving the Product' lend themselves to discussions about key aspects of team effectiveness.

Although I have specifically identified the 26 activities in this section as energisers' you might have noticed that many of the other activities in this manual can also be used for the same purpose - to invigorate the communication and teamwork of the group.

GO

Purpose:

Used as a pure energiser and group connection opportunity this activity is a lot of fun. It can also be used to emphasise some serious points about working in a group: e.g. pay attention to each other; stay alert about what is happening; respond quickly to the cues given by team-mates; stick to the process!

Process:

1. Participants stand in a circle with hands on hips, elbows touching (to indicate the right spacing)
2. The facilitator begins the game by demonstrating in slow motion. He or she makes eye contact with (and also points at) a person across the circle and simultaneously says 'GO' while walking towards them to take their place in the circle.
3. The person who is selected must look away (this is the hard bit!), make eye contact with and point to a different person and simultaneously say: 'GO' while vacating their space and walking toward the person they have selected to take their place in the circle.
4. As participants get the idea of the game, it will speed up. The facilitator can make the game more complicated and even faster paced by starting a second (or even third) 'GO' process.

Notes:

a) The key is to look away from the person walking towards you, point and say GO to another person <u>as soon as possible</u>.
b) Make sure you say GO as you start to move, NOT when you are 1 metre from the other person!
c) If the game breaks down into chaos, stop, explain again and re-start.

Reflective Questions

- What was the biggest challenge when playing the game?
- What did you learn about your ability to respond quickly under pressure?
- Was there a temptation to become a spectator? How is this related to our work as leaders?

The Jedi Mind Game

Purpose:
- Pure Energiser.
- A way of illustrating that attention can easily become overloaded.
- An illustration the subtlety of non-verbal communication.

Process:
1. All stand in a circle with one person in the middle.
2. The goal of the person in the center is to take another participant's place in the circle.
3. Participants in the circle attempt to switch places with another team member simply by making eye contact.
4. The eye contact should be as unobtrusive as possible so that the two participants can change places without either of them surrendering their place to the person in the centre. (Note: they must change with a person at least 3 places away from where they are standing).
5. The key to success in the game is to make eye contact with another participant, and to communicate non-verbally and with great subtlety that you want to switch places with them.
6. No talking or additional gestures can be used.
7. All players must attempt to keep changing places. Players who are noticed making no effort to move in any one-minute period are automatically sent to the centre.
8. The game continues until everyone has had enough!

Reflective Questions

No debrief required if the game is used as a pure energiser (one of the best!)

Debrief questions that may be used are:
- How difficult was it to establish eye contact without giving it away?
- What was the chief difficulty for the person in the centre?
- What was the most effective strategy and why?
- What did you notice about your ability to pay attention to everything that was happening?

Zip-Zop-Zap

Purpose:

Pure energy, with more than a touch of challenge to be as outrageous and loud as possible!

Process:

1. Everyone stands in a circle. The facilitator states that the aim of the game is for each person to receive and pass on huge balls of energy.
2. One person starts by clapping and pointing at another, while saying "ZIP" with as much vocal and physiological energy as possible.
3. The person who received the "ZIP" immediately claps and points at another, while saying "ZAP."
4. That person then claps and points to someone while saying "ZOP."
5. The pattern continues, "ZIP, ZAP, ZOP, ZIP, ZAP ZOP...." The goal is to pass the words and energy around as quickly and dynamically as possible.
6. It sometimes takes several tries to get into the rhythm of the activity Don't give up! Eventually, the group will begin to pass the energy on with a speed and a sense of team.

Variations:

- Insert 'BOING' to rebound the energy to the person who fired it at you, challenging them to pick up and continue.
- Initiate a second round of ZIP-ZAP-ZOP while the first is proceeding so that everyone has to be ultra-alert to the direction and rhythm of the next ball of energy fired at them

Reflective Questions:

- How does it feel to be constantly summoning a high energy state and maintain your focused attention?
- Is there a way in which we might use this as a useful metaphor for the demands on our leadership?

Change the Wheels

(An energiser inspired by the observation by Ted Sizer that 'changing anything in a school is like changing a tyre when the car is travelling at 100 km per hour!').

Purpose: As an introduction to discussion about any change. By introducing the topic in this way participants are more likely to be focused on the importance of introducing change empathically in a complex organisation.

Process:

1. Participants group in 4's, each forming the 4 wheels of a car.

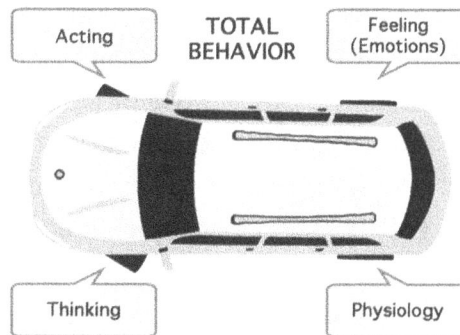

In this diagram, the four wheels of the Car are labelled according to Dr. William Glasser's designation of the four dimensions of human behaviour.

2. The 'cars' are given a 'track' to drive around, all travelling in the same direction. They must try to obey the commands given to them while still travelling as fast as they can while keeping the 'car' together.

3. The facilitator calls out commands in rapid succession:
   1. At 'switch' the left side wheels change with the wheels on the right.
   2. At 'change' the back wheels change with the front wheels.
   3. At 'rotate' all wheels rotate one position clockwise.
   4. At 'reverse' the wheels keeps the same positions but go backwards.
   5. At 'turn around' the car changes direction 180^0.

4. Continue as long as energy remains!

Reflective Questions:
- How does it feel to be overwhelmed by changes of process and direction?
- How is this understanding helpful to us when we are leading change in the school?

ZOOOOM

Purpose:
As a pure energiser & to illustrate the importance of focus and support, both as individuals and within the group.

Process:
1. Standing in a circle
2. One person begins by ZOOMING their attention to another person in the circle.
3. They use their hands and make clear eye contact to another person. The 'zoomer' places both of their hands next to their face, parallel to cheeks.
4. At the same time the people either side of the 'zoomer' become the support team. Whatever side of them is next to the 'zoomer' they raise that hand to their cheek so that for a moment there is a trio of people involved the 'zoom' across the circle.
5. Then the 'zoomer' points their hands to the person they have chosen and says ZOOM loudly and originally (your zoom should sound different to anyone else's zoom!) At the same time the two support-people on either side of the zoomer point to the team member who is being 'Zooomed'.
6. The person who received the zoom 'catches' it as if it was a ball, then moves hands up to place their hands to the face/cheeks and the people next to them place one hand to the face (the one next to the new 'zoomer'). Then 'zooms' to someone else.
7. You can use any word other than 'zoom'. (TEAM, SUCCESS, TOGETHER).
8. Continue as FAST and originally as possible.

Reflective Questions
- What was the most challenging part of this activity? (Usually the coordination of the 'zoomer' and the people on either side).
- How is this like the difference between being an initiator and supporter in the work we do together?
- In what ways is the power of focus vital to our work together?

Touch 4 Chairs (and infinite variations)

Purpose:
A simple and effective activity to create a change of 'state' and energise group members.

Equipment: whatever is in the room.

Process:
1. When the facilitator sees that individual or group energy levels are falling, call for attention and ask everyone to:
   'Touch 4 chairs' (one from each corner of the room) and return to their own place.
2. The variations are as abundant as the imagination of the facilitator (or group members) will allow. Some examples:
   * Touch all 4 walls of the room.
   * Find the person in the room who lives furthest from you.
   * Touch 6 elbows and a knee! (not your own).
   * Find out the favourite colour of 6 other people in the room.
   * Get into groups of 5 (like 'clumps') and share the most significant thing you heard/learned in the last 30 minutes.
   * High-five with 6 other people and create a secret handshake with one of these people.
   * Move around the room touching everything that is red.
3. In each case the instruction concludes with "and return to your own place". An element of competition can be implied or stipulated.

Note: when groups work together regularly, individuals can volunteer or be rostered to be the 'energiser bunny' and invent their own imaginative version of this activity.

Reflective Questions

* What happens to our attention and energy when we change thinking and physiology?
* What other changes did you notice before and after the activity?
* How might you use this in your work with your own teams?

Laneways

Purpose: Energiser, fun.

Equipment: none, but needs 18 participants or more.

Process:

1 Arrange 16 members of the group in 4 lanes and 4 rows:
The pursuer ⦿ in one corner, the fugitive ☺ in the opposite corner.

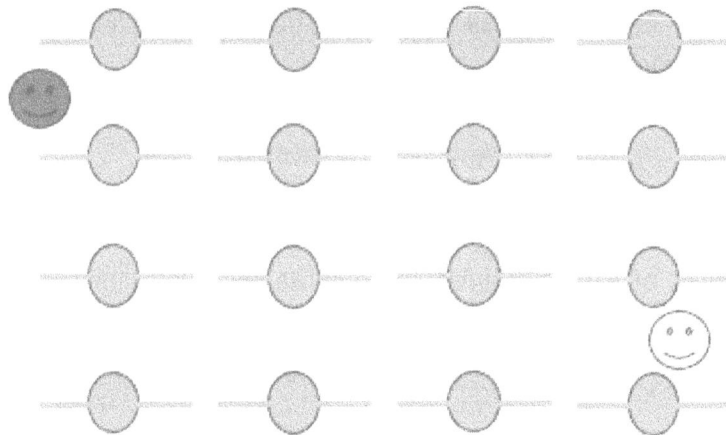

2 The participants stretch out their arms to form laneways, but at the call '**rows**' they swivel to create passageways at right angles to the laneways.
When '**laneways**' is called, participants swivel back to the original configuration.

3 The pursuer aims to catch the fugitive, but each can call out either '**rows**' or '**laneways**' to create or thwart the routes by which the pursuer can reach the fugitive. The participants who are forming the laneways and rows must count to 3 as they complete each new orientation and then respond to the next command (from either the pursuer of the fugitive) that they hear.

4 The game concludes when the fugitive is caught.

Reflective Questions
Can be related to the pursuit of a goal in a complex environment in which the parameters are ever-changing.

Magnets

Purpose: This is an energiser with a second purpose which is to enhance sensory acuity: participants are asked to remain aware of what is happening around them while at the same time being fully engaged in the activity.

Process

1. Participants are asked to silently choose two people as magnets in the room. One person has the opposite polarity to them (opposite poles attract) and the other person who has the same magnetic polarity (same poles repel).
2. Once everyone has covertly made their two choices inform everyone that their job is to get as close as possible to their 'opposite' pole (without touching) while moving as far as possible from their 'same' pole.
3. Begin the game.
4. After a few minutes the instruction is given for participants to reverse polarity - they then get close to the person they were previously distancing themselves from and 'repel' the person who they were formerly trying to get close to.

Reflective Questions

- Of course, everyone knows who they chose as their 'magnets'. But once the activity has stopped ask everyone to stand still and point to anyone who was either attracted to or repelling them. (in other words, who chose them).
- Discuss the sensory cues that people noticed in deciding who had chosen them.
- How can noticing these kinds of sensory cues help in the day to day work of teachers and leaders.

The Sun Shines On ....

Purpose: Pure energiser

Process:
1. Participant form a circle with one person in the middle.
2. The middle person says: "the sun shines on everyone ....." and chooses something that will apply to more than one person:
   a. "Everyone wearing blue";
   b. "Everyone wearing socks" etc.
3. Everyone who fits the description must change places with others to whom the description applies.
4. The person in the middle tries to fill a vacant place before those on whom the sun shines can change – leaving a new person in the middle ...

As the game progresses the person in the middle is challenged to find less and less 'visible' descriptions such as:
   a. "The sun shines on everyone who is an AP"
   b. "The sun shines on everyone who drinks beer"
And so on. The catch is that if the person in the middle announces a description that fits everyone – they stay in the middle!

Reflective Questions
   Not usually necessary.

Cross the Circle
(A variation of 'The Sun Shines On' – previous page)

Equipment: None - but a large open space is needed

Purpose: Energiser: but also useful early in the team's formation as participants will learn interesting information about each other.

Process: Participants stand in a circle with one person in the middle – the caller.

1. The caller identifies anything they would be interested to know about the others in the team or training group.

2. The other participants must cross the circle if they can answer positively that they identify with, have done, or can do whatever is identified by the caller. For example, the caller might say:
   - *"Cross through the circle if you have worked here more than 5 years;"*
   - *"Cross through the circle if you can play a musical instrument;"*
   - *"Cross through the circle if you live more than 50 kilometres from here;"*
   - *"Cross through the circle if you are an impulsive person;"*
   - *"Cross through the circle if you like to take risks;"*

3. If the other participants can positively identify with whatever is called they **must** cross the circle (that means they must go through the centre) and find an open spot on the other side left by someone else who also responded.

4. The caller takes the opportunity to fill a place left open by some-one who answered the question positively.

5. A new caller is left in the middle.

Reflective Questions:
Debriefing is optional. However, if the team leader notices that there are some interesting similarity or diversity, they might ask participants to discuss these in small groups and identify anything that is significant for the team.

TEAM Scissors-Paper-Rock

Equipment: None

Purpose:
A highly effective energiser that can also be used at the end of a day working together or the end of any extended period of team activity.

Process:
1. Participants pair off.
2. The facilitator demonstrates playing Scissors-Paper-Rock **with attitude!** Lots of competitive posturing and intimidatory scowling precedes the actual 1-2-3 Scissors-Paper-Rock contest.
3. Each pair stages a Scissors-Paper-Rock contest.
4. The loser of the contest between each pair falls in behind the winner (leader) with hands on their shoulders, and begins to cheer for them ("Go Rob, Go Rob GO" and "We are the Champions" etc.)
5. The winner, with their new 'team' attached goes in search of another winner to challenge. When a challenger is found their teams fall silent while the Scissors-Paper-Rock contest is held.
6. The losing team then becomes part of the winner's team and resumes the cheering.
7. When only two teams are left, the team leaders pair off for a best-of-3 grand final!
8. The losing team again falls in behind the winner - who makes a triumphant circle of the room with the whole team following behind and chanting victory slogans.

Reflective Questions

- What is the significance of finishing with everyone on the same team?
- How can we apply this principle to times when we are all competing for our own ideas to be adopted?

Fast Finger

Purpose: A quick energiser and interaction activity.

Process:
1. All stand in a circle.
2. All extend their left arm and put out their left hand, palm upward.
3. All extend their right arm and extend their index finger so that it hovers over the palm of the person to your right.
4. At the call of **finger**, every person tries to grab the finger of the person to their left while pulling their own finger away.
5. At the call of **freeze**, every participant remains still.
6. Score 1 point for each time that on the call 'finger' you successfully grasp the finger on your left **without** your own being grabbed.
7. Score zero if you grabbed the finger on your left but you own finger on the right was also grabbed.
8. Also score zero if your finger was grasped but you did not grasp the finger on your left.
9. Score minus-1 if you grasped a finger at the call of **freeze**!
10. The Winner is the first person to score 5.

Reflective Questions:
Not usually necessary though occasionally a discussion about who is and who is not competitive may be a useful team insight.

The Clap

Purpose: Energiser with concentration required

Process:
1. Form a circle and tell the group that the object of this exercise is to pass a "clap" round the circle as fast as possible.
2. The person who has the Clap must turn to face the person to whom the clap is going.
3. The nominated starter begins with one clap; second person can pass on the clap to the next person by clapping once;

    Or can clap twice to skip the next person;

    Or can clap hands, slap knees, then clap hands to skip two people;

    Or can clap hands in front, then behind, then in front to reverse the direction of the clap.
4. The Clap continues until it returns to the person who started it.

Note: it's usually best to start with a single clap and then keep adding the complications as the group becomes skilled.

Reflective Questions:
 Usually none required

Rope Tangle

Equipment: A rope that is long enough for all participants to hold it with a metre or so of space on either side.

Purpose: Energiser and group problem-solving. A good intro to a problem-solving meeting or training about problem solution.

Process:
1. While holding the rope with the right hand, stand in a circle.
2. All reach across the circle (still holding the rope with your right hand) and reach across with the left hand to grasp a free rope section.
3. The challenge of the group is to untangle the rope and stand in a line without letting go of the rope with either hand.

[This activity is similar to 'Human Knots', though participants in Rope Tangle are spared the close encounters with each other's personal space that 'Human Knots' requires!]

Reflective Questions:
- What does the activity remind us about problem-solving in our work life?

Butt Shuffle

Purpose: This is a surprisingly strenuous energiser that works best when the group knows and trusts each other already.

Equipment: Chairs in a circle. One chair for each participant plus one.

Process:
1. All participants sit together in a very tight circle without gaps between the chairs. It must be possible for participants to slide across to the next seat on either side without getting completely to their feet.

2. One person is randomly selected to stand in the centre.

3. The person in the centre attempts to find a seat on which to sit down again. Those already seated try to shuffle across on to the empty seat to close the gap – they are not allowed to use their hands to assist them*.

4. If the middle person succeeds in sitting down, the person who was too slow in shuffling across to close the gap is now in the middle.

[*Note that not using the hands to assist in shuffling across is a safety instruction. If a hand is being used to assist the shuffle the person in the centre can easily sit on it in their haste – very painful!]

Reflective Questions:
Usually not necessary

Budge

Purpose: An energiser that keeps everyone in a state of anticipation.

Equipment: Chairs - the same number of chairs as there are people playing – minus two. 20 or more people are needed to keep the game flowing.

Process:
1. Spread the chairs randomly around the room, facing in all different directions and with plenty of space between them.

2. Choose one person to be the chaser and another to be the escapee. Both Chaser and escapee must walk, not run.

3. Everyone else sits down on a chair. Start off with the chaser and escapee at opposite ends of the room.

4. The game begins with the chaser pursuing the Escapee. When either of them needs a rest, they can touch the chair of anyone who is sitting down and say "Budge!"

5. Anyone who is 'budged' must stand up and immediately assume the role of the chaser or the escapee (whichever 'budged' them).

6. If the chaser catches the escapee and taps them on the shoulder they swop roles.

7. You can complicate the game by having two escapees and two chasers (making it a real effort for everyone to keep up with what is happening!)

Reflective Questions:
The team leader can ask:
- What did it feel like to be in a constant state of readiness?
- Was it easier to be the chaser or the escapee?

Dragon's Tails

Purpose: An energiser that also introduces a reflection about risk .v. reward and self-protection.

Equipment: One Scarf or length of soft material for each person.

Process:

1. Everyone in the group tucks their scarf (the Dragon's Tail) into the waistband of their trousers or skirt.

2. Participants must move about the room without stopping. It's not OK to go within a metre of the sides of the room.

3. Every person tries to steal the 'Dragon's Tail' from another participant.

4. If you steal a 'tail' you must add it to the others tucked in at your waist.

5. If you lose a tail or tails you should try to steal replacements from other people.

6. NO violence please!

7. Continue for about 5-6 minutes.

Reflective Questions:

- What happens when you are focused on defending rather than accumulating?
- Who chose a risk-free strategy rather than attempting to take as many opportunities as possible?
- Who had the most fun – the people defending their tail or those focused on gains?

Take the Token

Purpose: As an energiser

Equipment: I counter, coin or token per person (a pebble or marble will also be OK).

Process:
1. Each person begins with one token or counter placed on the palm of their open hand and behind their back.

2. The hand can't be closed at any time during the game.

3. When the game starts, participants must keep moving by mingling with others in an unpredictable way.

4. The object is to surreptitiously steal as many counters as you can.

5. Multiple tokens can be stolen at one 'grab'.

6. If a token is knocked to the floor during a steal, it must be returned to the palm of the person who was holding it before the steal.

7. Any token you steal must be placed on your open palm with the tokens you already have and still held behind your back.

8. If you lose your token(s), you are still in the game and can continue to steal.

9. The winner is the person with the most tokens when the game is stopped.

Reflective Questions:
What could the tokens be a metaphor for?

Juggling

Purpose: To learn a new skill in the context of training and discuss the general principles involved. (The debrief is central to the activity!)

Equipment: 3 juggling scarves (or light plastic bags) for each pair of participants.

Process

1. Sit down on the ground. Start with two scarves — one on the ground to your left, and one in your left hand. Now throw the scarf in your left hand to the right and pick up the one on the ground. Repeat on the other side and you have the basic mechanics down.
2. Add the third scarf now. Hold two scarves and place one on your left side. Throw the scarf in your left hand, pick up the scarf on your left, throw the scarf in your right hand, pick up the scarf on your right. Throw, pick up, throw, pick up, etc. Eventually you'll be quick enough to throw and catch them while they hang in the air.

Note: You don't need to go buy special juggling scarves. You can use plastic supermarket bags since they're just as floaty and easy to snatch. Over time, you'll be able to move on to balls or bean bags using the same technique. When you're ready to stand and do it, or you're trying the heavier stuff, try standing over a table to make things easier.

Reflective Questions:

- What was the challenge of learning a new skill and practicing it while being watched by other people?
- Did the observers complicate the activity or make it more challenging?
- What insights does this activity offer for team learning, and for adult learning in general?
- How does a disparity in expertise or speed of learning affect the learning of adults? (or of students?)

BUZZ and BACK

Purpose: an energiser that is not physical but is good for re-setting the thinking of the group. Requires concentration!

Process:
1. Team members stand in a circle.
2. The leader announces the buzz and back numbers:
   E.g. 3 and 5 <u>or</u> 4 and 7 <u>or</u> 5 and 10.
3. The first person starts by saying "One." Starting to that person's left, each person will say either the next number in the normal counting sequence, or the word "Buzz," if the number is divisible by a designated 'Buzz' number or the word 'Back' if the number is divisible by the designated 'Back' number.
4. If the number is a 'Back' number, the direction of counting must reverse.
5. The leader gives an example by counting slowly around the circle when the designated numbers are 3 (buzz) and 5 (back):
   1, 2, Buzz, 4, Back, Buzz, 7, 8, Buzz, Back (and so on)
6. When a number is divisible by both Buzz and Back (e.g. 15 in the example above) the complication 'Shoot' is introduced.
7. When the number is a 'Shoot' number, the count is shot across the circle by pointing to someone and the counting continues to their left.

If someone in the group makes a mistake, the group starts the process over, with the person who made the mistake starting the new sequence with any number they choose.

Reflective Questions:
This activity, especially when used late in the day, illustrates how challenging it is to pay attention when we are tired.
- The leader may take the opportunity to introduce a discussion about how often we keep going when we are past our best or our thoughts are elsewhere.
- Does everyone have a personal strategy for refreshing their thinking and energy?

Improving the Product

Purpose: This is an energiser that can also be used as a discussion starter about how to work smarter.

Equipment: Cush balls, Juggling Balls or any soft ball.

Process:
[If there are more than 10 people in the team divide the team into 2 groups]
1. Give the group(s) one Cush ball or similar for every two people in the room.
2. Form a circle with participants two arms-length apart.
3. The group passes the ball around the circle, initially concentrating on passing on the ball so that it is easy to catch.
4. The team leader then begins to urge the group(s) to improve productivity (i.e. the volume of balls per second that move around the circle). However, participants can't do this by moving closer to each other – they must remain arms-length apart.
5. The team leader is measuring the group's ability to get a marked ball round to the starting point 5 times. If there are two groups encourage competition – otherwise measure the time taken.
6. If there are two groups the next level of the activity is for the groups to create points at which the balls are fed from one group to another and then back again so that one circuit for every ball involves being passed around the hands of both groups.

Reflective Questions:
Aspects of this energiser that can be used to de-brief the activity include:
- How did you improve the product? (Work faster / deliver more accurately / receive more carefully etc.)
- Did working faster introduce some complications? (Did group find that quality suffers as speed increases?)
- What did competition bring to the activity?
- What happened when the two groups had to interact with each other?

The team leader can lead discussion on how the 'findings' of the activity are significant for their work together or as team leaders.

No Smiling

Purpose: A simple energiser that encourages creative behaviours and usually produces lots of smiles!

Process:
1. Instruct everyone to stand and walk around the room making eye contact with others.
2. Everyone MUST keep a straight face and not smile under ANY circumstance.
3. Other facial expressions are allowed but NO SMILING or LAUGHING

Reflective Questions:
This simple activity usually provides the opportunity for discussion about:
*   The ineffectiveness of a negative instruction. The mind cannot process a negative.
*   The connection between **thoughts** and the other behaviours such as feelings, physiology and action.
*   Ways to intentionally use negative instructions with a paradoxical intention. E.g. Asking team members NOT to share their best ideas!

Crows and Cranes

Purpose: Pure energiser

Equipment: None - though best played in a space that has natural boundaries or with markers of some sort to delineate a border behind each player.

Process:

1. The leader lines up the participants facing each other in two lines, just far enough apart to not be able to reach out and touch hands. There should be a boundary of some sort behind each line.

2. One line is designated 'Crows', the other 'Cranes'.

3. Whichever name is called, the participants in that line have to try and tag the person opposite before they can escape to the boundary:
   E.g. If Crows is caused the Crows are taggers and the Cranes try to escape. If Cranes is called, the cranes are the taggers and so on.

4. The leader can heighten the suspense by saying "Cr..." and drawing out the first sound before completing it with 'ows' or 'anes').

5. A few rounds will usually suffice to energise the team.

Reflective Questions:

None required.

Brain Gym:

(I learned these two activities at a Mind-Gym workshop – presenter unknown)

Cross Crawling

Purpose: Cross Crawling is both energising and useful for enhancing the co-ordination between the left and right halves of the brain.

It is a very short but effective ways of re-energising quickly.

Process:
1. Participants stand in a circle so that they can work in the same rhythm;
2. Each participant lifts the right knee to touch the left hand at about waist height;
3. Then lift the left knee to touch the right hand about waist height;
4. The more deliberate participants are about crossing the midline of their body, the more effective is the process.
5. Continue in a rhythmic way (not fast) for one or two minutes.

Figure Eight Loops

Purpose: Figure eight loops is a relaxing break from concentration that is another way of establishing coordination between the left (logical) and right (creative) halves of the brain.

Process:
1. Participants stand upright with feet slightly apart.
2. Using either the left or the right hand with index finger raised, draw lazy, horizontal figures of eight in the air;
3. Follow the index finger with both eyes as it moves;
4. The Loops of the figure of eight should range from the centre-line of the body to about 30cm either side of the centre line on both left and right.
5. Continue for about 1 minute then change hands and draw the figure of eight in reverse direction.

Variation: the activity can be performed with a partner: one draws the figure of eight in the air and the other follow with the eyes. Take turns.

Blind Retriever

Purpose:
This activity is quite energising and potentially a little raucous if participants get into the spirit of the activity!
It can also be used to demonstrate aspects of teamwork and communication.

Equipment: Blindfolds and a soft ball or similar object.

Process:
1. Divide the group into 2, 3 or 4 teams.
2. Each team nominates one retriever who wears a blindfold.
3. The teams stand at the sides of the room with one team on each side of the room. Their blindfolded retriever stands in the corner of the room to the team's right, facing the corner.
4. The Team leader or facilitator begins the game by placing a soft ball or other soft object somewhere in the room (fairly central but not in the exact middle).
5. Teams must shout commands to their 'blind retriever' to steer them towards the object and to be the first to pick it up. As soon as the object is securely in the hands of one of the 'retrievers' that person shouts 'game over!' (No scrummaging for the ball is allowed!!).

   The game can continue with new 'blind retrievers.'

Reflective Questions:
- What aspects of teamwork were illustrated by this activity?
- When the retriever is hearing apparently conflicting messages what happens?
- What can this activity illustrate about the need for clear communication within teams or in the school generally?

Section Nine

Team Adjournment or Transition

Teams exist only for a time. In schools, teams are often seasonal: subject to the rhythms of the school year. As the year opens, new members come aboard to replace those who have followed new pathways. As the year ends, valued team members move on. And inevitably, there is the constant shifting and adjustment of membership created by staff leave, new appointments and the recasting of the team in response to events and need.

This section deals with team closures and transitions: the way to mark them, celebrate them - and learn from them. Material created in this adjournment phase of the team's existence can be 'paid forward' into the induction of new team members and in the regeneration of the team.

Some of these activities are reviews of various forms: their intention is to formalize reflection on past activity and make recommendations for the period ahead. Other activities are more celebratory in nature - their main purpose is to bring the work of the team to a temporary close through expressions of appreciation and gratitude for the contributions of those who have worked together as members of the team. And, of course, some of these activities include a measure of both these purposes!

Sometimes taking note of these transitions and temporary closures is neglected. In our rush to move on to the next cycle of team activity we too easily forget to say: "Thank You" and to elevate the importance of past achievements. It's a mistake to let this happen.

Far from being unnecessary, these opportunities to focus on endings before new beginnings form a critical part of team culture. As I argued in the 'Foreword' of this manual, team is always forming. Remembering to pause; to express gratitude; to recognise accomplishments and learn from them - these are as vital to the energy of the team as future plans and new intentions.

Because we are human, the emotion of appreciation and the celebration of what we have created together inevitably becomes the wind beneath the wings of the next iteration of the team.

History trip / Journey Wall

Purpose: To review and reflect upon the recent past, put it into context and provide a starting point for the new period. The end of the year is a good time to conduct this activity, but it can be useful whenever the team is in a period of renewal.

Equipment: Large Easel pads and 'Post-it' notes.

Process:
1. Decide on a period to review. It can be just the year past but there will be a better sense of context and continuity if a longer period is chosen – perhaps 2 to 3 years.

2. Put up blank easel pads with headings for each semester of the years chosen (as illustrated below).

3. Divide each easel pad into 3, each section representing:
   a. Events in Australian education;
   b. Events in the school & community;
   c. Contribution of the Team.

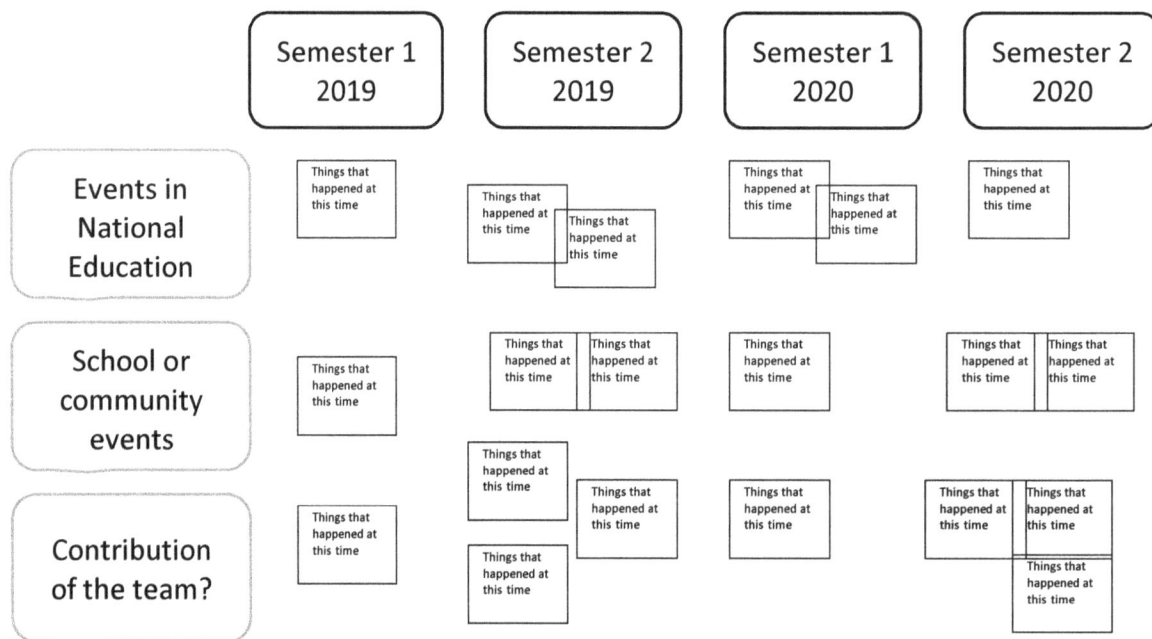

4. Individuals silently brainstorm events in all these 3 categories. Then working in small groups, write down significant events in all 3 categories on post-it notes.

5. Groups then put their post-its on the easel pads displayed on the wall, in the correct row and column.

6. When this is finished the wall should be covered by a large number of 'events' in each category.

7. The facilitator or team leader then ask questions such as these:
   - What relationships do you see among the events in different rows and columns?
   - Are there some 'chapters' that describe our work in various stages?
   - In which ways are we better equipped to improve teaching and learning now than when this team first came together?
   - What does the past suggest about our next priorities and where we should put our energy?

8. Now put up the next 2 (or more) semesters and ask groups to extend the journey into the ideal future: 'What will the next 2 semesters look like if we are to progress in our mission to be the best possible educators for our children during this time'.

9. Groups write new cards and add them to the wall for the future semesters.

10. Use this 'history trip' as a basis for discussion and future planning and share with new team members as part of the induction process.

Reflective Questions:
- What were you thinking about our work together before you viewed it embedded in context?
- What are you now thinking about our work together?
- How did reviewing the past year(s) make a difference to your thoughts about the future?
- If we use this review to induct new team members, which parts of our 'history trip' will you draw particular attention to?

The 12 Month Graph

Purpose: To review the past year, reflect on the team's highs and lows and use this to plan for the future.

Equipment: A large roll of paper on which a graph of team effectiveness (or whatever similar parameter is chosen) can be charted. The graph should have weeks on the horizontal axis and levels 1-5 on the vertical axis as illustrated below. It can be laid out on tables or pinned to a wall.

Process:
1. Team members bring diaries, the school calendar and any other records of the events of the past 12 months to the activity.
2. The team work individually to allocate effectiveness scores to the various activities of the team that belong in each of the following categories:
    1. Very effective decisions and actions;
    2. Effective decisions and actions;
    3. Decisions and actions by the team made little or no difference;
    4. Decisions and actions by the team with unintended negative consequences
    5. Decisions and actions by the team with unintended very negative consequences
3. Using a different colour for each team member, team members transfer their scores to the graph, allocating their numerical scores to a particular week or period (several weeks).
4. The Scores of each team member are joined making multiple line graphs (as illustrated – showing 15 weeks only):

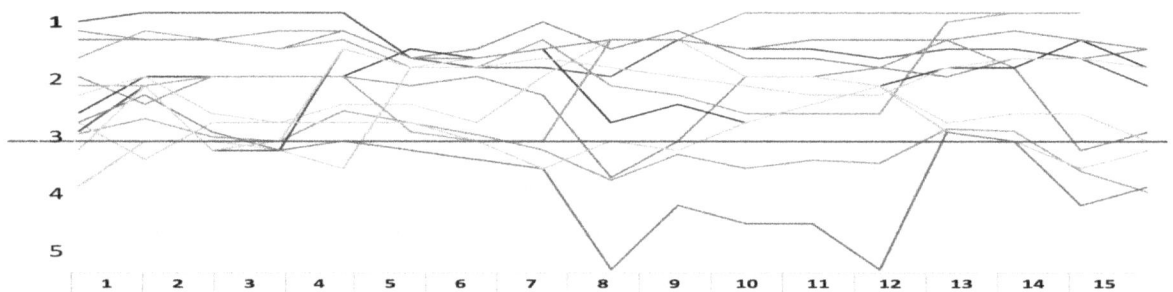

Reflective Questions:
- Were there large discrepancies between our scores? What are the reasons for that?
- Were there times when all of our scores dipped below or close to 3? What was happening then? How can we future-proof ourselves from these dips?

The Reflective Ramble and Review

Purpose:
Similar to the 'walk and talk' process in that participants walk in pairs but the conversation as they walk is focused on what each has learned from their experience as a team member.

Process:
1. The process is used during any team transition period and is particularly relevant when the team is reviewing the year past and celebrating its achievements.

2. Participants walk and talk using these prompts for their reflection:
    a. What have I learned this year?
    b. How have I grown as a team member?
    c. What do I know now, that I wish I had known before?
    d. Did I experience some mis-takes that I learned from?
    e. What would I like the new members of the team to know as we move into a new annual cycle?

3. The insights from the partner conversations can be shared with the whole team.

Reflection or review:

- What was common in our thoughts about the past year?
- What nuggets of wisdom will we take into the next year?
- How has each of us developed personally through our work together?

Learned - and Need to Learn

Purpose: To review the learning of the team – regarding both achievements and challenges; about how to work together; and about what skills or knowledge they would like to acquire in the year to come.

Process:
1. Working in pairs, team members ask each other these six questions:
   - What did you learn as an individual this year?
   - What did you lean as a team member (or as a leader) this year?
   - What did the team learn about how to be effective together this year?
   - What do you want to learn in order to be even more effective next year?
   - What do you think we need to learn as a team if we are to keep improving?
   - What would you like to be able to say about yourself and the team in 12 months' time?
2. Each pair now joins another. In groups of 4 team members make two lists:
   - the learning experiences they have valued in the year past (and which they would recommend for the future or for new team members).
   - The future learning that they believe will help team members - as individuals and the team as a whole.
3. The lists are shared with the whole team. Team members discuss what was common and what was particular to individuals.
4. A combined list of 'future learning needs' is drawn up.
5. With their original partner, team members work to allocate their priorities. They might also make specific recommendations about the time of year when a particular learning episode might be appropriate.
6. Priority lists are handed to a sub-committee who will draw up a recommended professional learning calendar for the team for the next 12 months.

Reflective Questions:
- Did some themes emerge, either in the lists of valued learning or in the list of needed learning?
- As new members join the team in the future, how will we bring them on board with the learning we have found most valuable in the past?
- Are there some learning experiences we can repeat and continue to draw value from?

Sails and Anchors

Purpose:
1. To identify the useful and valued aspects of the way the team works together in order to build them explicitly into the culture of the team.
2. To identify the features of teamwork and collaboration which are not yet working optimally so that these can be addressed in future.

Process:
1. Each team member is given a copy of the picture below, depicting a vessel in full sail, but encumbered by a variety of anchors and drogues.

2. On their picture, each team member writes on the billowing sails the aspects of teamwork and collaboration that are most helpful and important in the work of this team.
3. Similarly, team members write next to the anchors and drogues anything they think is inhibiting or hampering the effectiveness of the team and the cohesion of team members.
4. An A2 picture of the boat is posted on a whiteboard. Team members all transfer their individual comments to this master version.
5. The team is divided into 2 groups. One group works on the 'sails': the aspects of teamwork that are helping. The other group work on the anchors: the inhibiting elements.
6. Guided by the frequency of comments, but also by their own judgments of what is most important they create lists. The list created by the 'Sails' group is headed: **'Keep'**. The List compiled by the 'Anchors' group is headed **'Change'**. These 2 lists are used in forward planning.

Envelopes Full

Adapted from an activity by Thiagi.

Purpose: **As a celebration of work done together.**

Equipment: **A5 (or similar size) envelopes and about 10 slips of paper for each team member.**

Process:
1. Six A5 envelopes are prepared. Each has one of the following words written boldly on the envelope:

   > **Grateful;**
   > **Hopeful;**
   > **Peaceful;**
   > **Honoured;**
   > **Inspired;**
   > **Appreciative.**

2. Each team member writes, on the slips of paper, a note about team-related experiences, relationships, learning or conversations about which they are grateful, hopeful, peaceful, honoured, inspired or appreciative. The subject of each of the notes should be team related.
3. When the slips are completed they are placed in the envelopes.
4. The team sits in a circle and the envelopes are passed around the group.
5. As the envelopes are circulated, team members take on slip from any of the envelopes as it is passed to them. They immediately read whatever is on the note and then place the slip of paper on the floor in front of them.
6. Continue passing the envelopes and reading the messages until the envelopes are all empty.

If you like to end with some symbolism:

One team described how they then carry all the slips outside to a safe place and set them alight. As they watch the smoke rise and dissipate, the leader of the team talks about how the appreciation and ideas that they shared are now rising and spreading – waiting for them either in the new roles they take up or for the re-formation of this team.

Drum Ritual

Purpose: It's good to end the life of a team, or mark a team transition, with a noisy celebration. Drumming makes a lot of noise!

Equipment: If you have access to real drums **(or can afford to hire one of the many drum workshop groups)** so much the better. **However,** anything **that makes a noise will do**. I have heard this activity performed with team members:
- Clapping hands;
- Drumming on desks with palms or knuckles;
- Playing party kazzoos;
- Using tambourines or castanets;
- Clicking their fingers
- Using the back of a guitar as a drum;
- Clapping their thighs with open palms;
- Banging on pots, pans or trays;
- Stamping their feet on the floor.

Process:
1. The group works together to create drum beat rhythms that they believe symbolise the work the team has done together. This can be done all together or in small groups. It helps to have someone with musical 'nous' directing operations.
2. The rhythms created by the small groups are then assembled into a 'performance'. Ideally the performance will be created around a unifying beat, punctuated with brief 'solos' from every team member. A conductor is chosen to coordinate the performance and cue the solos.
3. After a few practices in which team members learn the performance the whole piece is played through with lots of affirmations and cheering after each solo.
4. To conclude the performance the team plays their team rhythm, over and over again, playing faster and louder each time. When they can play no faster the conductor direct the group to finish all together with three loud beats!
5. The atmosphere created provides a good opportunity for the team leader to say whatever 'thank you' or 'goodbye' messages that are appropriate.

Balloon Highlights

Purpose: To create a celebration of the team achievements of the past year. These achievements will include the improvements in the team's internal processes as well as the effects of team actions and decisions upon the school and wider community.

Equipment: A wide variety of large coloured balloons. Several wide-nib marker pens.

Process:
1. The team works in groups of 3 or 4, each with a selection of balloon and a marker pen.
2. The groups each brainstorm all of the highlights of the past year and write them down without critical analysis.
3. When completed, all lists are passed (clockwise) to another group who identify all of the highlights that they agree are worthy of note.
4. Each highlight is written on an inflated balloon as it is identified. As groups decorate a balloon with a highlight they <u>shout</u> it out so that other groups know that it has been recognised. All highlights that have been written on a balloon are crossed out on every list.
5. When groups finish with the list they have been passed, they pass it clockwise again so that another group review anything they believe should be recognised with a balloon.
6. If groups think of new highlights during the process they should check with another group and, if the group agrees, they add another balloon.
7. When all balloons have been decorated the job of the whole team is to clear a space, throw all the balloons into the air and then to keep all the inflated balloons in the air for at least 2 minutes. (Hard work if there are many more balloons than team members).
8. I like to finish the activity with a small glass of champagne for each person. Team members toast each other, the team leader congratulates everyone and when the meeting concludes everyone takes at least one balloon with them.

Gift Basket

Purpose: This activity creates a farewell presentation for those leaving the team. It's inexpensive, personal and usually far more memorable (and appreciated) than collecting a few dollars to buy a card or a box of chocolates.

Process:
Each team member thinks of some way to symbolise whatever they have appreciated in the relationship with the team member who is leaving. It can relate to something that you learned from them; something about their individual style or contribution to the team; something that you shared or had in common; or to the way that you experienced their support. The cost of the item should be trivial or non-existent, though occasionally a team member might contribute a book or a small gift because of its particular significance.

Example items from a farewell basket were:
- a smooth polished stone from the beach;
- a short poem;
- a page of inspirational quotes;
- a single flower;
- a photograph;
- a second-hand book;
- a soapstone carving;
- a notelet book;
- 2 chocolates (1 to eat, 1 to give away);
- a photo from a team dinner;
- a travel guide.

When the basket is presented, each team member says a very few words about what the gift they have provide symbolises or explains about their relationship with the departing team member.

The Album Alternative:
Another way of serving the same purpose is to create an album. On each page team members write something of significance, appreciation or thanks. This is a little more substantial and usually more meaningful than a 'card' with brief comments.

Big Shoes

Purpose: Designed to be used as a tribute to a team member who is leaving – as in 'you are leaving big shoes to fill!'. I know of one team that keeps a copy of the 'big shoes' as a reminder of the contributions made by former team members.

Process:

1. The outlines of two very large shoes outlines are drawn on a sheet of A3 paper (as illustrated). The Shoe shape can be chosen to be appropriate for the person who is leaving!
2. Team members write notes on the shoes describing the work the departing team member contributed to the team.
3. The notes written can refer to their leadership in the team; their commitment; their hard work; their support of other team members; their personal qualities or the fun and enthusiasm the brought to the team and its meetings.
4. The big shoes are presented with appropriate razzmatazz!

Note: Copies of the 'Big Shoes' could be shared with new team members to illustrate the level of commitment that is normal for the team. However, take care not to intimidate new team members!

Story Snowballs (or 'whose story'?)

Purpose: Team transitions are often stressful for team members. This activity emphasises team unity and team members acquired understanding or each other; it also celebrates the degree of knowledge each has acquired of their team colleagues.

Process:

1. Each team member prepares a story that illustrates something about their experience of working with the team through the year OR something that they think they have learned during the year.
2. The 'story' may be one they have read or heard, a true story about something that happened, a metaphorical or allegorical story, a fairy tale or anything else that the team member thinks is appropriate.
3. The story should be written on a single sheet of paper which must be crumpled up into a loose paper ball.
4. When the team leader says 'share stories' every paper ball is thrown up in the air.
5. Every team member picks up a ball of paper that lands near them.

> Variation: Team members can write their story on a slip of paper which is rolled up and placed in a coloured balloon. All the balloons are thrown in the air and team members attempt to keep all the balloons aloft for 2 minutes. At the end of that time everyone picks up a balloon (of a different colour from their own), bursts it and extracts the story.

6. Team members read out the story they have picked up. When the story has been read they discuss who they think chose that story and the clues they used to identify the person (it's amazing how often they will be right!).
7. The team member who did contribute the story can add a few comments about what the story means to them.
8. Continue until all the stories have been shared.

Fortune Cookies

Purpose: A good humoured celebration event that also enhances team ties and contributes to the team's narrative about itself.

Process:
1. Each team member provides two *anonymous* contributions to the final team meeting:
   - 5 to 6 'cookies' to be consumed at the team meeting. The 'cookie chosen must in some way represent the person who brings it. (E.g. firm but with a soft centre; very sweet; crunchy). Team members can have a little fun deciding what to choose as their 'cookie'. *(Note that the 'cookie' can be a lolly, a cake or anything else that is sweet and can be eaten at the meeting).*
   - The 'fortune' which should be a catchphrase, pithy piece of 'wisdom', proverb or slogan must appeal to the person who contributes it. It should be the sort of thing that they might say or quote in the appropriate circumstances.
2. The contributions should be left in an appropriate place well before the meeting so that no one can be sure who provided what.
3. When the meeting begins the 'cookies' are displayed on the meeting table and every team member randomly takes one of the 'wisdom' sayings.
4. Team members take it in turns to read the 'fortune in front of them. When each fortune has been read, the job of the team is to decide (guess?) which team member contributed it.
5. When the contributing team member has been correctly identified, the team guess which cookie he chose to bring (and why they identify with it).
6. The activity proceeds, usually with lots of laughter, until everyone has been identified and all of the cookies eaten!

Whoosh!

Purpose:
You can use this activity to punctuate the last meeting of the team before a transition such as the end of the year.

Process:

1. Team members stand in a circle.
2. The team leader says: "Imagine we are all standing here holding a huge net. The net has handles all around it. Please take the hand of the person next to you and imagine that you are grasping those handles".
3. The team leader continues: "Now imagine that in that net are all of the things that we have achieved together; all of the hopes and dreams we have shared – both those fulfilled and those still waiting to come to fruition. Place in the net everything we have learned together, and everything we still yearn to learn."
4. "Now, on the count of three, I want us to throw up our hands and 'whoosh' the net and its contents up into the air so that they will be waiting for us when we convene again."
5. The team leader counts 'one' and team members swing arms forward and up and then back (still holding the 'handles' of the net). On the count of 'two' they again swing forward and back. Finally on the final swing up everyone shouts **'Whoosh'** and releases the 'handles' of the net – letting go all of the things they have imagined until they are ready to take them up again next time the team meets.

Using Energisers and other Activities
- for Team Adjournment

In addition to the fourteen Team Adjournment and Transition Activities listed in this section, some energisers and other team activities in the book can be used at this point in a team's lifetime.

Team Scissor-Paper-Rock is a boisterous and energising activity to mark team transitions or closure. It starts with 'competition' but ends with everyone on the same team cheering for the same person.

Zip-Zop -Zap and similar games can provide a high energy finish with team members invited to hurl the energy they have accumulated around the circle.

Balloon Up can be modified into a closure activity in which team members work in a really coordinated way to keep all the balloons in the air. When played this way the emphasis is on communication and mutual support.

Other closure Activities that might be considered are:

My Advice In this activity team members bring one sage piece of advice which mean a lot to them to share. Every team member chooses on piece of advice to take away.

Ball of Yarn (Wool) In which participants express appreciation to a team-mate who then expresses appreciation to a different person. As the Yarn is thrown it unravels and team members keep hold of the yarn when they throw it. The activity continues until the ball of wool is unravelled allowing everyone to see the complex network of appreciation that remains.

Drawing to a conclusion (adapted from a Thiagi suggestion). Individually. team members draw their positive experience of the team and then interpret each other's pictures.

Arrived back where he started. Saw it for the first

FutureShame Consulting

A perplexing situation. A surprising result!

FutureShame Consulting

He thought he was superior. What does that make me?

FutureShame Consulting

The one who wins is the person who thinks they can.

FutureShame Consulting

Finding out what I stood for. Having something to say.

FutureShame Consulting

The sea. Sailing away. Returning another way.

FutureShame Consulting

Time and Chance - happens to all.

FutureShame Consulting

Unheard cheering. Silences deafening.

FutureShame Consulting

Caring for others. Caring for me. Where is the balance?

FutureShame Consulting

He was very ordinary, nothing exceptional. Catching happiness?

The Sea.
A boat.
Stars.
Rocks.

What achieving means to me. What failing means to me. What it means to be me

Labelled as incapable. What happens next?

My first leader. My worst leader. Where did I learn to be me?

The kids are bored. It's their fault.
My job is to teach!

Winning. Bigger and more important races. Losing inevitable.

A river flowing. A life's journey. A happy ending?

Fitting in. Not fitting in. Feeling important. Feeling irrelevant. Finding my way.

I still make coffee
for two.

Life is a hard game
to play. Where do
I find the rules?

Fooling everyone.
Some of the time.
All of the time.

It's not all my
fault. Not always.

First I listened to what
they thought of me.
Then to what I
thought of them.
Then to what I think

My dad knows
nothing. Time
passes. He's
learned a lot!

Once I was. Now
I'm not. Who am I
now?

Is it forgive and
forget, or forget
and forgive?

He did not listen
to me. He thought
I did not care.

Passengers, this is not your Captain speaking.

Ring. Church. Groom. Anyone missing?

Strangers. Friends. Best Friends. Love. What next?

The ring I brought, I never should have.

Friending. Making friends. Being a friend.

They lived happily ever after, separately.

Stronger. Faster. Higher. Is that all there is?

I did ask to live backwards.

Old books. Old ideas. New discoveries.

Looking old.
Feeling young.
Life's
conundrum!

It's our fiftieth. A
table for ten
please.

Worth fighting
for?
The important?
The nonentity?

Afraid of
becoming like my
mother.

Sorry soldier.
Shoes sold in
pairs.

Love the person,
hate the
commitment.

A familiar voice.
Wrong number!

Deaf friend says
"You are too
quiet"

Which comes
first: alcohol,
decision,
consequence?

www.ingramcontent.com/pod-product-compliance
Lightning Source LLC
Chambersburg PA
CBHW080249030426
42334CB00023BA/2747